Guidelines

VOL 26 / PART 2
May–August 2010

Commissioned by **Jeremy Duff**; *edited by* **Lisa Cherrett**

Suggestions for using *Guidelines*

Set aside a regular time and place, if possible, when you can read and pray undisturbed. Before you begin, take time to be still and, if you find it helpful, use the BRF prayer.

In *Guidelines*, the introductory section provides context for the passages or themes to be studied, while the units of comment can be used daily, weekly, or whatever best fits your timetable. You will need a Bible (more than one if you want to compare different translations) as Bible passages are not included. At the end of each week is a 'Guidelines' section, offering further thoughts about, or practical application of what you have been studying.

You may find it helpful to keep a journal to record your thoughts about your study, or to note items for prayer. Another way of using *Guidelines* is to meet with others to discuss the material, either regularly or occasionally.

Occasionally, you may read something in *Guidelines* that you find particularly challenging, even uncomfortable. This is inevitable in a series of notes which draws on a wide spectrum of contributors, and doesn't believe in ducking difficult issues. Indeed, we believe that *Guidelines* readers much prefer thought-provoking material to a bland diet that only confirms what they already think.

If you do disagree with a contributor, you may find it helpful to go through these three steps. First, think about why you feel uncomfortable. Perhaps this is an idea that is new to you, or you are not happy at the way something has been expressed. Or there may be something more substantial— you may feel that the writer is guilty of sweeping generalisation, factual error, theological or ethical misjudgment. Second, pray that God would use this disagreement to teach you more about his word and about yourself. Third, think about what you will do as a result of the disagreement. You might resolve to find out more about the issue, or write to the contributor or the editors of *Guidelines*. After all, we aim to be 'doers of the word', not just people who hold opinions about it.

Writers in this issue

Chris Tilling is the New Testament Tutor at St Mellitus College and St Paul's Theological Centre, London. His present area of research concerns the apostle Paul's understanding of the identity of Christ.

Jenny Hellyer is a spiritual director, musician, clergy wife and mother based in Oxford. After teaching and theological study, she was part of the Lee Abbey Community in Devon for seven years.

Jo Bailey Wells currently teaches at Duke Divinity School in North Carolina, USA, where she also serves as Director of the Anglican Episcopal House of Studies, preparing able young leaders for ministry. She also teaches regularly at Renk Theological College in Southern Sudan.

Jeremy Duff is Director of Lifelong Learning in Liverpool Diocese and Canon at Liverpool Cathedral, as well as being the Commissioning Editor for *Guidelines*. His latest book, *Meeting Jesus: Human Responses to a Yearning God*, was published by SPCK in 2006.

Dick France is a retired Anglican minister who taught New Testament for 26 years. After serving as principal of Wycliffe Hall, Oxford, he spent several years as Rector of seven small parishes on the Welsh border. He has written substantial commentaries on Matthew and Mark.

Henry Wansbrough OSB is a monk at Ampleforth Abbey in Yorkshire. He is Executive Secretary of the International Commission for Producing an English-Language Lectionary (ICPEL) for the Roman Catholic Church, and lectures frequently across the globe.

Andrew Goddard is Tutor in Christian Ethics at Trinity College, Bristol, where he is helping develop a Centre for Bible and Society. He also edits *Anvil*, the Anglican evangelical journal for theology and mission, and serves on the leadership team of Fulcrum.

Michael Tunnicliffe is a freelance tutor in adult education in the northwest of England.

Volker Rabens teaches New Testament at Ruhr-University Bochum, Germany. He is the author of *The Holy Spirit and Ethics in Paul: Transformation and Empowering for Religious-Ethical Life*.

Further BRF reading for this issue

For more in-depth coverage of some of the passages in these Bible reading notes, we recommend the following titles:

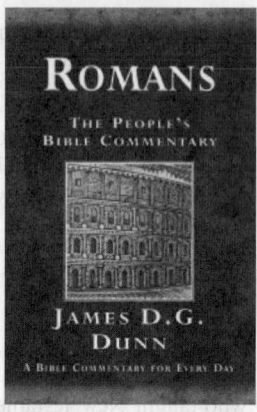

978 1 84101 082 3, £8.99

978 1 84101 151 6, £8.99

978 1 84101 070 0, £7.99

978 1 84101 047 2, £7.99

The Editor writes...

'Therefore, I urge you, brothers and sisters, in view of God's mercy, to offer your bodies as living sacrifices, holy and pleasing to God' (Romans 12:1, NIV). This is our goal as we seek to follow Jesus and help others, also, to encounter God. It is a challenge that Paul has to 'urge' the Romans to take up. It relies on our grasp of 'God's mercy', living in response to God, not in an effort to gain favour with him. It is worked out in our everyday lives and our bodies as 'living sacrifices'.

This edition of *Guidelines* brings us to the heart of these issues. We begin and end with expositions of the first half of two of Paul's letters—Romans (with Chris Tilling) and Ephesians (with Volker Rabens). Both will be completed in the next edition. Both letters open our eyes to the greatness of God's mercy. Romans wrestles with the 'big picture' of what God has done; Ephesians declares to us the spiritual blessings we have received. In between, Dick France guides us through the theme of 'Atonement', helping us grasp the richness of the biblical imagery for God's great act of mercy achieved through the death of Jesus Christ.

Other contributions focus on the question 'How shall we live?' This is asked explicitly in Andrew Goddard's notes on 'Biblical ethics and Christian discipleship'. In a different way, it is also at the heart of 'Being people of the Spirit' by Jenny Hellyer. Our lives of discipleship are empowered and shaped by God's Spirit. Our study of Ezra, guided by Michael Tunnicliffe, engages with the same issue. How were the Jew-

ish people to live within the Persian Empire? (This study has been adapted from Michael's PBC volume on Chronicles to Nehemiah.)

All scripture challenges us, but the challenge is particularly focused in our studies of 'Isaiah and the nations' and Luke 7—10. In the former, Jo Bailey Wells explores how Isaiah was called not just to receive the good news of God's mercy, but to take that message to the nations—a challenge that has been passed on to us as the Church. In Luke 7—10, the next instalment of our Gospel for this year, Jeremy Duff faces us with the challenge to respond to Jesus' teaching, to Jesus himself and to God.

Finally we begin a new series on the Psalms with Henry Wansbrough. This will be a constant thread through the next years of *Guidelines*. Through the Psalms we will share the pains and joys of God's people as they take up the challenge of responding to God's mercy with sacrificial lives in God's service.

The BRF Prayer

Almighty God,
you have taught us that your word is a lamp for our
feet and a light for our path. Help us, and all who
prayerfully read your word, to deepen our
fellowship with each other through your love. And
in so doing may we come to know you more fully,
love you more truly, and follow more faithfully in
the steps of your son Jesus Christ, who lives and
reigns with you and the Holy Spirit,
one God for evermore. Amen.

Romans 1—8

In 1545, Martin Luther mused upon his 'conversion' experience, describing himself as 'a sinner before God with an extremely disturbed conscience'. But upon reading a text in Romans 1 he started to understand the righteousness of God not as a threat but as the means by which 'merciful God justifies us by faith'. He then felt he had 'entered paradise itself through open gates'.

Many readers, though, find that Romans rather slams these gates shut! To help open them again, it will prove most useful to keep in mind the place of Christ's life, death and resurrection in the story of Israel. This is important as Paul may well have been trying to answer a different (even if overlapping) set of problems to those generated by Luther's 'extremely disturbed conscience'.

The bumpy narrative of the Old Testament scriptures runs from creation, fall, the covenant with Abraham, through Egypt, the exodus, conquest of the land, the judges, the monarchy and the Assyrian and Babylonian exiles, and ends with a partial, yet incomplete, restoration. Yet the Old Testament prophets had spoken of a time when God's redemptive plans, through Abraham's family, would be fulfilled—when God would make a new covenant, pour out his Spirit, raise up a messianic leader, reunite the twelve scattered tribes, establish his people in the land and glorify his name (see, for example, Isaiah 43:5–11; Jeremiah 16:14–16; Ezekiel 36:19–28; Zechariah 8). The centuries leading up to the New Testament period did not see the fulfilment of these promises; instead, Israel suffered the rule of one foreign empire after another. So, many asked when God would be faithful to his covenant with Abraham. And what was God to do if his chosen people continued to break covenant?

The phrase 'God's righteousness', which brings us to the heart of Romans, expressed the expectation that God would indeed be faithful to his promises. Yet, as we shall see, God's righteousness, in the sense of impartial justice, was also the reason why they went into exile in the first place. This tension in God's righteousness generated difficult questions, exactly the sort Paul sought to address in Romans, albeit with a special Christian twist: the righteousness of God is revealed in the life, death and resurrection of Jesus in such a way that God is both impartially just and faithful to his covenant.

Let us, then, begin the journey into the letter itself. These notes are based on the NRSV.

1 Introducing the gospel of God

Romans 1:1–15

In about AD57, probably from Corinth, Paul wrote this, the most famous of all his letters. In Paul's day it was customary to start a letter by stating the identity of the sender and then to name the addressees. But before he manages to proceed beyond a statement of self-identification, mention of the 'gospel' launches him, in verses 2–4, into a more detailed description of that gospel, a major theme in Romans. It concerns God's Son, declared to be messianic Son of God through resurrection. Resurrection runs as a crucial thread throughout Romans, giving Paul's argument focus and shape.

The title 'Christ' ('anointed one') *denoted* being a 'descendant of David' and 'Son of God'. It *connoted* the specific story of Israel and what God 'promised beforehand through his prophets in the holy scriptures' (v. 2). The meaning of Jesus, for Paul, is all about the Jewish story found in what we call the Old Testament. Separated from these moorings, Romans can drift into all manner of potentially anachronistic waters, in which the gospel becomes, for example, solely about 'me and Jesus and how I get to heaven'.

It is in this Old Testament story that the word 'gospel' finds its home. It reflects language in Isaiah 40:9 and 52:7, which speak of the redemption of Israel and the return of the tribes from exile. These and other scriptures suggest that when God acted to restore his people, the Gentiles would in some way benefit from (or at least witness) God's salvation (see, for example, Psalm 67; Isaiah 60:1–9). This important scheme can be outlined as follows: exile/judgment → restoration/redemption → light to Gentiles.

Likewise, Paul turns from his description of the restoration theme of the gospel of God to his apostleship, which aims 'to bring about the obedience of faith among all the Gentiles' (v. 5). It is time for the Gentiles to hear of salvation. Already we can see that Romans needs to be read in light of the story of Israel outlined in the introduction.

After a greeting, the ancient letter form turned to thanksgiving. Likewise, Paul offers a thanksgiving prayer in verse 8, developing into a statement of his eagerness to come to Rome. He wants to 'reap some harvest' (v. 13).

2 The theme of the letter

Verses 16–17 build on Paul's opening statement of the gospel and briefly state the theme of Romans. They really belong to the introduction, to 1:1–15, but in important ways they also lead into the section on idolatry and consequent human depravity starting in 1:18. To see why this is so, we need to look at Habakkuk, from which Paul quotes in verse 17, and see how it illuminates the disputed language of 'righteousness' in this passage.

In Habakkuk, God responds to the sins of Judah by sending the Chaldeans against them (1:1–11), but the prophet complains in bewilderment: how can you judge your own people for their wickedness by sending an even more wicked nation against them (1:12—2:1)? The answer comes: with the Chaldeans marching against Jerusalem, the righteous will live by God's faithfulness (or their own faith: there are two main versions of this text), and await the judgment that will ultimately also be unleashed against the Chaldeans (2:2–20). God will not simply overlook his people's sin. He will be *impartial*. Yet they remain his covenant people, so he will also be *faithful to his covenant* to his people, to save them and judge their enemies. The righteous will live by faithfulness.

Habakkuk is all about the question of what, in Paul's Greek, is *dikaiosynē theou* (v. 17)—God's righteousness. Although not all scholars agree, this could indicate God's faithfulness as well as his impartiality in judgment. Habakkuk displays the inherent tension within God's righteousness between his covenant faithfulness to defend and uphold Israel, on the one hand, and divine impartiality to judge sin, on the other. We should expect to find the same, then, in the developing argument in Romans.

This link with Habakkuk is one important reason why the other possible translation of the Greek *dikaiosynē theou*, '… a righteousness from God' (NIV), is less likely than that found in the NRSV. Paul's world of thought is all about the question of *God's own* righteousness. The gospel that Paul proclaims is God's power for salvation precisely in this context. This redemption and outworking of God's righteousness is for all who have faith, as in Habakkuk—first to the Jew but also, for Paul, to the Gentile. All of this summarises the centre of Paul's concerns in Romans and, like all shorthand summaries, it may initially cause some confusion. How the tension inherent in God's righteousness, faith and Christ all relate to each other will now be developed, but to do this Paul must turn to the problem to which Christ is the solution—sin.

3 Pagan idolatry and human corruption

The link with Habakkuk and God's judgment on Israel and the nations helps us to see why Paul speaks about faith in the context of the wrath of God being revealed against ungodliness (1:18). This wrath is revealed because all deserve it; everybody is without excuse. Gentiles know the revelation of God in 'the things he has made' (v. 20), but instead of giving him honour they turned to idolatry (vv. 21–23). This leads to the important equation, typical of Jewish anti-pagan rhetoric at that time: idolatry leads to human depravity or, as Paul puts it, being 'given up' to sin (vv. 24, 26, 28). The focus on homosexual practice is used not to say that this is the worst sin but to indicate that a world turned from God to idolatry is ultimately unnatural, a clear sign of the distortion of humanness resulting from the deeper problem of idolatry. After all, human genitals are designed for heterosexual intercourse. Sin is, thus, about living in a way that falls short of God's design and intention for a full human life.

This also means that God's wrath in these verses is not simply about a grumpy despot in heaven. It reflects, rather, God's redemptive concern for his creation to be liberated, a theme that awaits further and powerful development in Romans 8.

In the first few verses of Romans 2, Paul explains that no one can stand aloof from this judgment of humanity, to be revealed without partiality to Jew or Gentile (v. 11). The style of Paul's language is known in classic works from the ancient world as 'diatribe'. He anticipates the potential objections of imaginary opponents, responds to them and thus helps his readers think through the correctness of his position.

Ironically, though, Paul's language in 2:6–16 has caused much confusion. If Romans is supposed to be all about justification by faith apart from works, why does Paul seem to claim the opposite? It is not the hearers but 'the doers of the law who will be justified' (v. 13). The answer may lie in understanding these 'doers', in contrast to Jews who break the Law, as Gentile believers who fulfil the the Jewish Law (compare 13:8) through faith in Christ and by the power of the Spirit. While future judgment seems to be, in Paul, according to the way Christians have lived—that is, by works (2 Corinthians 5:10)—how this relates to justification by faith apart from works in the present (Romans 3:28; 4:6) remains a matter of controversy. But the passage's concern is first and foremost to establish the impartiality of God, a necessary characteristic for a righteous judge.

4 Israel has also failed

Romans 2:17–29

Jewish texts from around the time of Paul could describe pagan idolatry as the cause of the fracturing of human society, the root problem. Paul in these verses makes the same argument, but with a twist. It is not just the Gentile world but the Jewish one, too, that is under sin. At various points, Paul has already hinted in this direction, especially in 2:9–10, but now the matter is stated explicitly.

In verses 17–20 Paul lists the covenant privileges enjoyed by Israel. Called to be a blessing and a light to the nations (see Genesis 12:3; Isaiah 42:6), they know a unique covenant relationship with God, they possess the Law and are 'a light to those who are in darkness' (v. 19). A set of rhetorical questions in verses 21–23 drives home his point: Jews are no better than Gentiles. Of course, when Paul writes, for example, 'You that abhor idols, do you rob temples?' (v. 22), he surely means that such sin is to be found in Israel, not that every Jew robbed temples! But the matter is clear: these guides to the blind have become part of the problem. Sin is in their midst, too.

His argument ends (v. 24) with a citation from Isaiah 52:5, a text that thematically reflects other Old Testament passages such as Ezekiel 36:17–23. These prophetic texts explain how the people of God went into exile because of their unfaithfulness. Instead of being the light they were intended to be, thus addressing the problem of the fall (notice how the call of Abram in Genesis 12 follows immediately after the fall and its consequences in Genesis 3—11), God is blasphemed because of his people. The cycle of idolatry and human societal corruption, as described in the previous section, is thus deepened by Israel. As it is written, 'The name of God is blasphemed among the Gentiles because of you' (v. 24).

As suggested above, Paul has already begun to speak of the new covenant believer in 2:6–16. Now he loops back, in verses 25–29, to that Gentile person in a way that redefines Jewishness. It is not about external rites, such as circumcision, but about a change of heart. This 'spiritual Jewishness', he will go on to explain, characterises all those who are 'in Christ', whether ethnically Jewish or Gentile.

5 The theological problem of Jewish unfaithfulness

Romans 3:1–20

If a person can be a Jew 'inwardly', surely there is no advantage to being ethically Jewish. Paul raises precisely this question in verse 1 and answers it, 'Yes, there certainly is advantage'! The pace of Paul's argument can be difficult to follow at this point, but the point is clear: the advantage lies in having been entrusted with the oracles of God, with a redemptive message for the world.

Paul's previous argument leads to a deeper problem, though. Recall the discussion above about a potential tension in God's righteousness—between righteousness as impartiality and as covenant faithfulness to his people. The sin of Israel raises a theological problem: how is God to fulfil his plan of blessing the world through his chosen people if those people are also part of the problem? Does not Israel's unfaithfulness mean that God must judge them and not bless the world through his people? Again Paul answers in the negative: 'Will their faithlessness nullify the faithfulness of God? By no means!' (vv. 3–4). In verses 4–9, Paul, again in the form of diatribe, notes and briefly answers the problems raised by an unfaithful Israel in terms of God's faithfulness, wrath, justice (or righteousness), truth, judgment and glory. He will return to these questions in more depth in Romans 9—11.

Paul has already made much of God's impartiality: indeed it was the *leitmotif* of most of Romans 2. He is about to explain how God is also true to the associated aspect of his righteousness, namely faithfulness to the covenant. He has already stated his answer very briefly in 1:17, but now he is ready to explain in more detail how God is righteous to his covenant.

Before Paul can make his primary point about God's covenant faithfulness revealed in Christ, however, he must first establish the crucial point of his argument more firmly, now that all potential objections have at least been anticipated in verses 1–8. In 2:17–29, when Paul had begun to detail the sinfulness of Israel, he looped his argument back to a discussion of Gentile believers in Christ who fulfil the Law. Now, however, he puts this important matter of the sinfulness of Israel beyond dispute, and he does it by listing a number of biblical passages, which all point to the same conclusion: the Jew is, just like the Gentile, under sin (vv. 9–20).

6 God's righteousness revealed

Romans 3:21–31

The question now emerges: how is God to be righteous? Given the sin of Israel, how is God to be both impartial (the essence of the righteousness of a judge) yet also righteous in the sense of being faithful to his covenant to his people?

Two more features need to be grasped before Paul's answer to these questions can make sense. First, as Israel's Messiah, Jesus *represents* Israel. When King David sinned, trouble came upon the entire nation (1 Chronicles 21:1–7). When David fought Goliath, on the other hand, he won for all of Israel. Just as the entire people of God could be called the son of God (Exodus 4:22), the king himself was also called son of God (Psalm 2:7). In the same way, Jesus, the Davidic Messiah, acts as Israel's representative.

Second, the Greek translated 'faith in Jesus Christ' in verse 22 can be translated as 'the faith *of* Jesus Christ' (see NRSV footnote)—that is, 'the faithfulness of Jesus'. Given the flow of thought in the first chapters of Romans, a case can be made to prefer the alternative reading. So in verse 22 Paul writes of 'the *faithfulness of Jesus Christ* for all who believe'—not Jesus' faith in God, but something effectively synonymous with Christ's 'obedience' (see 5:19).

Paul's argument should now come into focus: God's righteousness is disclosed through the faithful obedience of Jesus Christ. Because Christ was faithful as Israel's representative, God's covenant faithfulness can now be revealed without contradiction by God's righteous impartiality, which would necessarily judge sin. Whereas Israel had been unfaithful (3:3), leading to God's name being blasphemed among the nations (2:24), Christ was faithful (3:22) and as such he represented the covenant people. Therefore, now God's covenant purposes to bless the world through Abraham's seed can finally flow to the Gentiles.

Verses 21–26 are not a complete 'doctrine of atonement'. Yet Paul does use sacrificial language to explain the redemptive significance of Christ's death, in terms of the revelation of God's righteousness. In his death, Jesus turns the wrathful consequences of God's impartiality from his people: he dies *for* them (v. 25). Because of this, God's righteousness is 'shown' (v. 25) or 'proved' (v. 26). All who believe, Jew and Gentile, find in Christ the representative, which means that they themselves are justified—that is, established 'in right relation' with God and with others in the believing community. In relationship with Jesus the theological problems raised in 3:1–8 are thus solved.

Guidelines

Understanding Paul's letter to the Romans is an exercise in intellect, but it is also a test of our character—perhaps in an unexpected way. When we relate with other people, we want to be, as James 1:19 puts it, 'quick to listen, slow to speak'. We want to learn the skill of listening to other people without immediately imposing our own presumptions and judgments. This first week of our overview of Romans is all about learning to listen. Of course, instead of hearing another person, we are reading a text, but the dynamic is very similar. So a question arises: can we allow Paul's reasoning in Romans, which may seem foreign and almost unintelligible to us, to 'have its say' before we leap on the text and make it fit our own theological boxes? Can we dare to think through Romans as if Paul were not necessarily trying to answer all of *our* immediate questions? Can you list a few ways to cultivate the art of better listening to the New Testament?

Notice that Paul, in Romans 2:16, says that God will judge all 'according to my gospel'. This may strike many as rather odd! How can judgment itself be a part of the good news? Is it not judgment from which we are saved? What might Paul's claim here mean for our own understanding of God's judgment?

1 The promise to Abraham

Romans 4

In the last verses of Romans 3, Paul asks, 'Or is God the God of Jews only? Is he not the God of Gentiles also? Yes, of Gentiles also' (3:29–30). Of course, God's covenant with Abraham was that the Gentiles would find blessing through God's chosen people (Genesis 12:3; Isaiah 49:6). Abraham was called to deal with the problem of Adam for the nations.

This background helps to explain what is going on in Romans 4. But before this is elucidated, a note on the translation of verse 1 is necessary. The original Greek manuscripts did not include punctuation; hence a debate arises about how it should be read. While most Bible versions propose a different reading, a good case can be made for the following translations: 'What then shall we say? Have we [Jewish and Gentile Christians] found Abraham to be our forefather according to the flesh?' Must Gentiles become Jewish to be justified by God? Understood in this way, Romans 4 continues with the theme ending Romans 3.

The three main points then discussed by Paul are works (vv. 2–8), circumcision (vv. 9–12) and law (vv. 13–15), but not directly in the sense that these things indicate a Jewish legalism contrasted with faith. Rather, all of these points engage the question in verse 1 about the scope and nature of Abraham's family. Paul turns to Abraham not as an illustration of justification by faith (the NRSV slightly misleadingly titles this section as 'The example of Abraham') but because the calling of Abraham was about the nations.

The story of Abraham makes clear that his being counted righteous (Genesis 15:6) was not on the basis of works, circumcision or law, but through faith by grace. This righteousness is of faith, thus basing it on God's gracious initiative and making it available to all. This faith, whether for Abraham or Christians, Jew or Gentile, is resurrection faith in God who raises the dead (4:17, 24). The blessing of Abraham comes to the nations through Christ's faithfulness, and so God is faithful to his covenant *in Christ*. We can notice, for example, how idolatry and sin in 1:18–32 are reversed in 4:18–25. The problem of Adam is dealt with in the (Abrahamic) covenant through Christ, a point that Paul will develop in Romans 5.

2 God's love: from Adam to Christ

It is generally agreed that Romans 5—8 forms a distinct unit within Romans, as did Romans 1—4. In those first four chapters Paul's argument was a little abstract, rarely speaking to the Roman Christians directly. Now he turns his attention to those believers and starts speaking more often of 'we' and 'you'. This means that 3:21—4:25 constitutes only the groundwork of Paul's answer to the problems raised in 1:18–3:20, which needs further elaboration in Romans 5—8.

Some scholars think that an important Old Testament narrative lies in the back of Paul's mind throughout Romans 5—8: (1) God makes a covenant with Abraham to deal with the problem of Adam. (2) His descendants end up in Egypt. (3) They are later delivered from slavery in Egypt and go through the Red Sea. (4) They are led to Sinai and given the Law (Torah). (5) They eventually obtain their inheritance, the promised land.

This hypothesis at least explains the shape of Romans 5—8. Now you and I are included in the promise of Abraham, through Christ, dealing with the problem of Adam (5:12–21). We too go through water for deliverance from slavery—not the Red Sea but the water of baptism (ch. 6), and not from Egypt but from slavery to sin. Paul, like the exodus narrative, goes on to speak of the law (ch. 7) and finally the inheritance (ch. 8), though not of land but of the whole cosmos.

In Romans 5:1–11, Paul explains that what God has begun he will bring to completion (see also Philippians 1:6). Having been justified and reconciled (past), we have peace with God, we hope and we suffer (present) as we await salvation and rescue from wrath (future). Just as those who left Egypt would indeed enter Canaan, these Christians will leave the Egypt of sin and will assuredly inherit the glory of God, a renewed cosmos.

Paul further develops lines of thought expressed in Romans 3:24–26 to explain the basis for this hope, namely the deliverance won in Jesus Christ, as Christ's death shows the unshakeable love of God. If that is so, 'how much more' can we be assured that God will finish what he has begun (vv. 6–11).

Verses 12–21 contrast Adam with Christ, directly developing the line of thought from Romans 4 and the discussion concerning Abraham. As blessing to the fallen world was to come through Abraham, here we see how God's covenant commitment is accomplished in Christ. Righteousness— right standing with God in covenant community—is a free gift, the result of an abundance of grace found in Christ. The basis for this is Christ's 'act of righteousness' (v. 18) or 'obedience' (v. 19), which parallels Paul's language of the 'faithfulness of Christ' in 3:22.

3 Baptism and freedom

Romans 6

Romans 6 consists of two sections, both beginning with a question: 'Should we continue in sin in order that grace may abound?' (v. 1) and 'Should we sin because we are not under law but under grace?' (v. 15). The first question arises because of the two 'dominions' mentioned in the previous chapter (see 5:21), the dominions of death and righteousness. Paul's response first draws on the language of baptism, and the basic logic runs as follows. Just as it is true that Christ died and was raised to life, this is also true of those who, through baptism, are in Christ. Therefore, Paul answers in verse 12, 'Do not let sin exercise dominion in your mortal bodies'.

How does this work? We have already seen that, as Israel's Messiah/ Christ, Jesus represents Israel. 'In Christ', what is true of him becomes true of his people: Christ's faithfulness becomes Israel's faithfulness. Through baptism we are 'in Christ', and so Christ's death and resurrection become our death and resurrection.

But this carries with it an imperative: as this is true of those in Christ, we must behave accordingly. 'We have been buried with him by baptism into death' (v. 4) becomes 'So you also must consider yourself dead to sin and alive to God in Christ Jesus' (v. 11). For Paul, the statement (vv. 1–10) is the basis for the command in verses 11–14, as is generally the case in his letters.

These imperatives lead into the second half of Romans 6: verses 15–23.

In particular, the mention of 'law' (which, unless there are clear indications otherwise, always means 'Torah' for Paul) leads to the second question. In this section the language of slavery is prominent. One the one hand, it speaks of slavery to sin—not merely one's private sin but rather sin as a cosmic force opposed to God. The Adamic link to sin in Romans 5 puts it on the map of Genesis 3—11, as the dissolution of the social and moral fabric of humankind. On the other hand is slavery to God/righteousness. Paul's question makes clear that Torah belongs to the dominion of sin. If baptism reflects the theme of the new exodus, as it does in 1 Corinthians 10:2, then Paul indicates that the new exodus in Christ does not lead to Sinai and the Torah, but to a new wilderness generation marked out by its relationship with Jesus through baptism.

4 Torah and the Christian

Romans 7

After the deliverance through the Red Sea and the wilderness journey, the Israelites were brought to Sinai. So if Christians are delivered from slavery through the waters of baptism, are they too simply brought back to Sinai and Torah? How does Torah relate to Christians? What is its significance?

Again Paul draws attention to the theological significance of the death of Jesus. In his analogy from marriage he points out that the Torah is only binding until death. Yet if we are in Christ, the death of Christ frees us from the law. Once again, what is true of Christ becomes true of us, so 'we are discharged from the law, dead to that which held us captive' (v. 6).

How could Paul say such a negative thing about the Torah? Surely Psalms like 119 make clear that Torah was something to be enjoyed? The Old Testament narrative suggests an answer. When God gave the Torah, Moses prophesied that Israel would indeed fail to keep it (see Deuteronomy 27—30). They would thus inherit the 'curse of the law', meaning the wrath of God, which would send them into exile and death. Paul has already made the case, in Romans 2, that Jews too are under sin and have been faithless, leading to the defaming of the name of God in exile. In other words, Torah belonged to the time of exile and wrath and served only to emphasise sin; now we need to be 'discharged' from it.

Paul makes clear in verses 7–12 that the Torah itself is not to blame. The fault lies with the sin within Israel (those who possessed the Torah). Yet Paul does not say 'Israel' but uses the first person singular (7:7–24). For centuries the Church has debated whether this language refers to life as a Christian or life before baptism and faith. Undoubtedly, Paul movingly portrays the sort of struggle with sin that many Christians experience, yet it can also be argued that he uses 'I' as a rhetorical device to express the story of Israel under sin. This solution would at least explain the nature of Paul's analysis of Torah: it belonged to the time before Christ and resulted in exile and judgment. The matter is not about human feelings but eras and epochs, with the coming of Christ bringing redemption. So this chapter ends: 'Who will rescue me from this body of death? Thanks be to God through Jesus Christ our Lord!' (vv. 24–25).

5 Spirit and life

Romans 8:1–17

Romans 7:6 was quoted in yesterday's reading. Paul continues in that verse to say, 'We are slaves not under the old written code but in the new life of the Spirit', and this theme is picked up in more detail in Romans 8:1–17. An important background to Paul's argument is found, again, in the narrative of the Old Testament. God had promised through the prophets that when he acted to fulfil his covenant promises, return his people from exile, raise up a messianic leader, rebuild the temple and make his people a blessing to the nations, not a blasphemy, *he would pour out his Spirit* and give his people a new heart to obey his Torah (for example, Ezekiel 36:26–27). As we saw, Paul now says in Romans that God has fulfilled his promises (see also 2 Corinthians 1:18–20) and demonstrated his covenant faithfulness in Christ (Romans 3:21), which must mean that, because of Christ, the Spirit is poured out in fulfilment of these prophetic promises.

By sending his Son and condemning sin in (his) flesh, God has demonstrated his impartial justice and thus made it just to keep his covenant promises. Hence 'the law of the Spirit of life in Christ Jesus' sets us free 'from the law of sin and of death' (v. 2). Through the Spirit 'the just requirement of the law might be fulfilled in us' (v. 4), and the mind set on the Spirit is 'life and peace' (v. 6)—both central aspects of God's covenant promises now fulfilled in Christ through the Spirit (see Isaiah 54:10; Malachi 2:5). This is why 'anyone who does not have the Spirit of Christ does not belong to him' (v. 9).

Just as the wilderness generation was led to their inheritance of land by a cloud in the day and by a fire at night (Deuteronomy 1:33), now this new exodus people is led by the Spirit of God. The wilderness generation were tempted to fall back into the land of slavery (Numbers 14:3–4), and this new covenant people 'did not receive a spirit of slavery to fall back into fear' (8:15). They have received a renewed intimacy with God through the Spirit (v. 16), led to be heirs not of a strip of land on the eastern side of the Mediterranean but of the whole world (vv. 17–23).

6 The hoped-for inheritance

Romans 8:18–39

Christians are those, Paul seems to say in Romans 6—8, who are brought through the waters of baptism from slavery to sin because of the saving death of Christ, and are led by the promised Spirit to their inheritance, 'the glory about to be revealed' (v. 18). This inheritance is not merely the land 'from the river of Egypt to… the river Euphrates' (Genesis 15:18), but the renewed cosmos.

When many Christians speak of their 'inheritance', meaning 'heaven as separate from the created world', Paul's argument in Romans is a necessary corrective. Through the sending of the Son and the power of the Spirit, God will make sure that 'the *creation* itself… will obtain the freedom of the glory of the children of God' (v. 21). Just as Abraham was called to be a blessing to all the families of the earth, so creation is not rejected by God, destroyed or forgotten in Paul's gospel. It is rather redeemed and set free to experience its own exodus from bondage.

'Not only the creation,' Paul adds, 'but we ourselves… wait for adoption' (v. 23). Again, this has nothing to do with the popular notion of 'going to heaven when we die'. Paul expressed that great goal of adoption as 'the redemption of our bodies'—of our *bodies*. The physicality of Paul's hope can sound rather odd to some, especially those of us raised on hymns such as 'How great thou art', with lines like 'When Christ shall come with shout of acclamation, and take me home, what joy shall fill my heart!' A theology inspired by Paul is more likely to sing '… and heal creation, what joy shall fill my heart!'

Until that hoped-for day, the Spirit 'helps us in our weakness', and 'all things work together for good for those who love God'. Not only that, but those whom God called 'he also justified; and those whom he justified he also glorified' (vv. 26–30). This is the necessary assurance for Christians who, still in the wilderness, await the inheritance. The theme of justification, so prominent in Romans 1—4, is here linked with the theme of sharing in the future glory, surfacing in Romans 5—8 (see 5:2; 8:17–18, 21). Being established in right relation (justified) leads to the assured future of a redeemed world and our part in it with redeemed bodies. The basis for all of this (verse 31 perhaps refers back to the whole argument of the letter thus far) is the love of Christ, from which nothing can separate us (vv. 31–39).

Guidelines

Abraham was central to Paul's argument in Romans 4. The same is true in his letter to the Galatians, where he writes that God 'declared the gospel beforehand to Abraham' (3:8). If Abraham is key to understanding what the gospel is, what might this mean for our understanding of it? What might it mean, in light of Paul's use of Abraham, to claim that we preach the gospel?

The scope of Paul's gospel is such that it embraces me, my personal life, my sin and my future. But it is also larger than this: for Paul, the hope of the gospel is for all creation. What might Paul's gospel mean, then, for matters such as physical health and environmental issues? In this light, for what sort of things might the Spirit want to help us to pray (see Romans 8:26)?

Throughout Paul's argument, especially Romans 5—8, God's love has been strongly emphasised. Indeed, it is the basis and foundation of God's activity in Christ and by the Spirit. The cross shows us not just an abstract theory of atonement but the glowing love of God for us 'while we were still sinners'. It shows the abounding, unrestrained kindness of God's free gift, of gracious mercy and redemption in Christ. And all of this love is directed to us. Try to list four practical ways that will help you, in the coming week, to enjoy, experience afresh and relax in this unbounded love of God.

Being people of the Spirit

We begin to enter the mystery of the Holy Trinity, not so much through philosophical or rational explanation as through Christian experience. During the next two weeks, we will be looking at the character of God expressed through the Holy Spirit, and at how we can become people of the Spirit, exhibiting the fruits and gifts that he freely bestows on those who recognise their poverty and are ready to be changed.

Each day there will be an opportunity to respond to the text, taking your reflections into prayer or into an exercise that may help you allow the gracious work of the Spirit to take place.

In preparing these reflections, I have been struck both by the power of God—for example, in creation and at Pentecost—and by the love that the Spirit invites us to experience and to give away.

'I pray that out of his glorious riches he may strengthen you with power through his Spirit in your inner being, so that Christ may dwell in your hearts through faith' (Ephesians 3:16–17).

Unless otherwise stated, quotations are taken from the New International Version of the Bible.

1 Creator Spirit

Genesis 1

These days we are accustomed to global news and the capacity to see what is happening almost anywhere on the planet. The ancient text we look at today is global too, and has the feel of an epic tale. You might like to read it aloud.

In the beginning, the Spirit of God was instrumental in the unfolding acts of creation described here. He was 'hovering over the waters' (v. 2) like a bird that provides for and protects its young. He helped bring form to earth's formlessness (vv. 3–10); he was part of the making and filling (vv. 11–25) that removed emptiness. The pinnacle of his task was the creation of humankind, made 'in the image' of God himself; verse 27 is the first example of poetry in scripture.

Proverbs 8 is a hymn that personifies Wisdom, also involved with God in creation (see especially vv. 22–31). As in the Genesis account, there is 'rejoicing in his whole world' and a particular 'delighting in mankind' (v. 31). Both accounts, Genesis and Proverbs, find their fulfilment in the New Testament, which clearly points to Christ's work in creation: 'For by him all things were created… in him all things hold together' (Colossians 1:16–17)

What does it mean to bear God's likeness or image (Genesis 1:27)? It means that every human being is worthy of respect; it means that we can carry the characteristics of him who loves us—holiness; the capacity to love, create and be life-givers too.

See what follows on from the piece of poetry in verse 27: 'God blessed them…' (v. 28). God's primary desire and instinct is to bless us with fruit-fulness, significance, creativity and relationship.

Take a moment to reflect that the work of the Spirit is rooted in the love of God; he is good. He expresses the goodness of God. Remember that God's great desire is to bless. What is the benediction he wants to give you today? In the quiet, be open to receiving his blessing. You might like to open your hands on your lap as an expression of your trust.

2 Identity

Isaiah 44:1–5

From the unfathomable events at the beginning of time, we turn to a passage that speaks of the Creator's relationship with his people. We do not worship a God who 'set the clock going' but then stood back; here we see the intimate and ongoing involvement of the Lord both individually (v. 1) and corporately (v. 3). 'Israel' is both one person and a whole nation. Notice the tenderness of God's words to Jacob/Israel: he was part of his servant's formation in the womb; he knows the fragility of human experience, dispelling fear (v. 2).

Out of this intimate knowledge and care comes a promise of his Spirit, to be poured out: 'I will pour out my Spirit on your offspring, and my blessing on your descendants' (v. 3). The two parallel phrases in this verse are interchangeable in Hebrew meaning, so we can truly understand that God's outpoured Spirit is his blessing, his goodness given as an ongoing gift down the generations. The image of healthy, luxuriant growth (v. 4) is a delightful one—an image of abundant life, not mere survival.

See what the outworking of the Spirit's touch is on us: 'I belong to the Lord' (v. 5). The Spirit knits our identity to God himself: as Paul puts it, 'The Spirit himself testifies with our spirit that we are God's children' (Romans 8:16). Our core identity in this world is that we belong to the one who made us and loves us.

The second part of the Spirit's work is to enable us to see our kinship with others: 'another will call himself by the name of Jacob' (v. 5). We belong to God's community, to one another.

Isaiah looks forward to the time when the Spirit will enable a transformation of both individuals and whole cultures. This is a beautiful and hopeful text—one to ponder, within which you might find yourself, too.

Perhaps you would like to meditate on the intimate knowledge that God has of you, and on how you belong to him and to others. What difference might this make to the way we relate to ourselves and to others?

3 Spirit of truth

2 Samuel 12:1–25

Nathan was a trusted prophet to King David: when David had it in mind to build a house for God, in the manner of other cultures of that day, it was Nathan who sought God and delivered his word and purpose to David (2 Samuel 7:2–17). In consulting a prophet, a leader was seeking God's will.

So, in our passage for today, Nathan would have had David's ear as he spoke one of the most poignant and powerful parables of the Old Testament, which foreshadows those of Jesus himself. The prophet's use of story engages at an emotional as well as an intellectual level, and so provokes a heartfelt response from David.

Nathan shows remarkable courage in challenging the king with the truth about his deceit, and David shows great humility in accepting it (v. 13): notice that he does not seek to justify himself in any way.

When God confronts us with truth, his intention is to bring repentance, freedom and restoration rather than condemnation and despair. Perhaps this principle is helpful in discerning the difference between God's truth and other people's damaging criticism?

This episode in David's life concludes with the birth of Solomon, who is given the prophetic additional name Jedidiah (meaning 'loved by the Lord'). Nathan—the same man who had previously brought challenge—delivers this assurance of God's favour. Grace has the last word.

In our lives, too, we need the Spirit to bring truth to bear on our motivations and decisions. Like David, we sometimes need correction, and God may speak through image or story in order to release genuine change.

Take a few moments to reflect. Is there something troubling you? Bring it to God, however small or great it may seem. Like David, know that God wants you to move on, knowing forgiveness as his gift. Do you need to forgive yourself? Remember that beautiful name: 'loved by the Lord'. Receive this name for yourself.

'Let the beloved of the Lord rest secure in him' (Deuteronomy 33:12).

4 Mary welcomes the Spirit

Luke 1:26–38

Mary was a descendant of yesterday's character, David the king of Israel. The Spirit is at work in her life in a very different way, however.

In Genesis we read of the Spirit hovering over the world as God spoke creation into being. Here we find similar imagery: 'The Holy Spirit will come upon you, and the power of the Most High will overshadow you' (v. 35). God is bringing about a new creation—this time, astonishingly, through one of his people. Luke makes it clear that the conception of Mary's baby is the work of the Spirit.

The 'favour' (vv. 28, 30) that Mary is given will soon show for all to see—a pregnancy. The work of the Spirit is not always comfortable. Mary will know the discomfort, the social disgrace, of expecting a child out of wedlock; later she will experience the death of this son in the most brutal fashion. Yet such is her availability to God at this moment that she can only concur: 'May it be to me as you have said' (v. 38). She trusts.

If you read on, you will notice how the Spirit touches Elizabeth's unborn child and Elizabeth is 'filled' (v. 41). Then her exclamation releases prophetic praise in Mary (vv. 46–55). The Holy Spirit has caught up these two women in the great and glorious purposes of God.

Mary's was a unique encounter. Her 'yes' to God facilitated our salvation. Although her calling was so costly, she was empowered (the *dunamis* pronounced by the angel Gabriel, v. 35). Later, as Jesus was dying, he provided her with another 'son' to take care of her (John 19:26). In her discipleship she was sustained.

We may fear the 'favour' of God if it is to be costly, but this is the call to each of us. It is an invitation to live in the great and glorious purposes of God.

In quiet, reflect on your own experience—the sense of God's call, the cost at times, but also the joy and privilege and the knowledge of being empowered and sustained. Are you available to be an instrument of the Spirit, whose desire is to bring life?

'I am the Lord's servant' (v. 38).

5 Jesus and the Spirit

Mark 1:9–13

The promise of Isaiah 44 is beautifully fulfilled in this moment in the life of Jesus. The Spirit comes and the Father speaks a personal, affirming word to him: notice that each member of the Trinity is here.

In asking to be baptised, Jesus consecrates himself to God, identifies with those around him, and is presented as Messiah by John, his cousin. Later, at the synagogue in Nazareth, he will quote Isaiah 61:1–2a, suggesting that he sees the descent of the Spirit as the moment when he was equipped for his ministry: 'The Spirit of the Lord is on me, because he has anointed me to preach good news to the poor. He has sent me to proclaim freedom for the prisoners and recovery of sight for the blind, to release the oppressed, to proclaim the year of the Lord's favour' (Luke 4:18–19).

Alongside the equipping, however, this moment forges Jesus' identity as beloved Son, a delight to his Father: it is a window for us into an intimate relationship. The dove-like Spirit suggests gentleness and purity. It is a holy experience, both for the Messiah and for us as we contemplate a God like this—tender and loving.

If the Spirit forges identity and equips for ministry, he also leads us into desert places (vv. 12–13) in order that faith and character might be established. This experience of testing was no less comfortable for Jesus than it is for us today. For Jesus, his status both as Son and as Messiah was challenged by the temptations he endured (see the fuller account in Matthew 4:3–11).

Today's reading seems to bring together strands that we have already met this week: the Spirit portrayed as a bird, the primacy of relationship, and God's call, empowering and sustaining us through challenges.

You may like to pause and reflect on verse 11: 'You are my son/daughter, whom I love; with you I am well pleased.' God's love is a given: it is not dependent upon our effort or on any ministry that we offer. Take one of the phrases in this verse and see where it takes you; let your meditations form a prayer.

If you find yourself in a desert, remember that, like Jesus, you are being forged and refined. Like him, may you experience divine protection and, in days to come, a godly ministry.

6 Jesus promises the Spirit

John 14:15–27

There is an intensity to these words of Jesus, given as he ate a last meal with his beloved disciples, knowing what lay ahead. Notice how Father, Son and Holy Spirit are all woven into this passage, each engaged in giving the most wonderful gift to us. Jesus knows that the Father will give what he requests (v. 16), even as Jesus is about to give what the Father has asked of him—his own life. We see the loving surrender among the three persons of the Trinity; astonishingly, Jesus invites us into this way of life, as this is what we are made for.

As Jesus promises the gift of the Holy Spirit, he assures his disciples, 'I will not leave you as orphans' (v. 18). Both Father and Son will 'come… and make our home' with them (v. 23). The Holy Spirit is given so that we might know our deepest identity as people who are at home with God.

Our part is to obey (vv. 23–24, literally to 'keep' commands). To follow the ways of God, with the help of the Spirit, is our expression of love, just as it is within the Trinity. There is a work for us to do! God gives his creatures the dignity of choice; he gives us the best teacher (v. 26) and counsellor (v. 16)—also translated 'advocate' (NRSV), literally one who stands by to defend and assist. As God keeps us in his love, we keep responding to the promptings of the Spirit and to Jesus, the living Word. This duality of love and obedient response is beautifully expressed in Psalm 119:32: 'I run in the path of your commands, for you have set my heart free.'

Christians down the ages have discovered the joy and the cost of being people of the Spirit. Like Jesus, we will be called to lay down our lives, perhaps in small daily responsibilities or perhaps in more dramatic ways—but our reward is to know God (v. 21).

Take a moment to be open to the loving Holy Spirit. Remember that he is a gift to you, to assure you that you belong to God. Breathe in and out slowly a few times as a way of allowing yourself to surrender to him. Peace is his gift, so let go of fear and any troubling worries. Let him fill you and indwell you, as Jesus promised. Stay, receiving what the Spirit wants to give you, and thank him.

Guidelines

In our reflections on the people of the Spirit, we reach a day in the church calendar that has been described as the birthday of the Church: the Day of Pentecost. It's not usual for the 'Guidelines' section to include a Bible passage, but you may wish to look at Acts 2:1–12 on this special day.

As the Spirit fell, the disciples spoke in the many languages of the large crowd present for the festival (vv. 8–11). God's desire to reach all with his love could not be plainer. His intention was to reveal Jesus to them: this is what the Spirit loves to do. There are echoes here of our reflections on identity in Isaiah 44, as the Spirit of blessing is poured out. And yet, the drama of violent wind and tongues of fire reveals another dimension of the Creator Spirit—his sometimes unpredictable power that defies human understanding.

The expectancy and obedience of the early followers of Jesus led to the birth of the Christian Church and mission, in the power of the Spirit. God has no different strategy today. He took the disciples into his agenda, the purposes of his love for the world. He will do the same for us.

The biblical characters we have met this week—Isaiah, Nathan, David, Mary, John the Baptist—were willing to be a part of his strategy in the different places where he put them. As these ordinary people drew near to God, he drew near to them. Are we, too, willing? Are we, like them, empowered and sustained? Wait, as the first disciples waited in Jerusalem (Acts 1:4), and ask for his loving power to fill you.

'If you then, though you are evil, know how to give good gifts to your children, how much more will your Father in heaven give the Holy Spirit to those who ask him!' (Luke 11:13).

1 Spirit-filled preaching

Acts 2:14–41

Where did this Galilean fisherman learn such boldness and such an ability to communicate the gospel? If you read parts of this passage aloud, you will sense the vibrancy and immediacy of Peter's speech. You will also realise that he is very aware of his Jewish audience, preaching as he does from their scriptures.

His first intention is to explain that the outpouring of the Spirit is the fulfilment of Old Testament prophecy and a sign that the messianic age has come. Then he centres everything on Jesus (vv. 22–36). The resurrection of his crucified Master has led to the Father's promised gift of the Holy Spirit, whose power is evident for all to see.

This account of Peter's first 'sermon' stands as a remarkable model for preachers and for all of us who seek to be communicating the gospel to friends and family. Remember that Peter has been filled with the Holy Spirit: such preaching and response is only possible in God's strength. Can you see parallels, too, with the story of Nathan and David? This is another example in which the Holy Spirit gives courage to the speaker and repentance to the hearers, leading to forgiveness. In this passage we see how the Spirit emboldens, equips, convicts, brings people to Jesus and builds a new community.

Read the passage again, slowly, allowing a phrase or word to be high-lighted as you do. Stay with this phrase, reflecting upon it, and see where your thoughts lead you. Turn your reflections into simple prayer, expressing what is on your heart and mind.

You might like to pray this prayer (of Søren Kierkegaard) for your own local community of God's people:

Holy Spirit, you make us alive;
bless also this our gathering, the speaker and the hearer.
Fresh from the heart it shall come, by your aid;
let it also go to the heart.

2 An act of kindness

Acts 3:1–10; 4:8–14

Luke describes here an incident during the early days of the infant Church. It has immediacy: we are caught up in the encounter between the two disciples and the crippled man, and we delight in the 'walking and jumping, and praising God' that follow. It all happens out in the street, so it has a huge effect both on passers-by and on the temple authorities.

As I write, there is a controversy in the UK about Members of Parliament and their expenses: we feel cheated when power is abused. However, in this account before us, we see a different kind of power. The power of the Holy Spirit releases compassion—an act of kindness (4:9). Furthermore, this power brings freedom and healing.

Does the Spirit work through us just as he did through Jesus and through Peter? Our great commission is to make disciples, to baptise and to teach them to obey everything Jesus commanded (Matthew 28:19–20), and such prayer for healing is being restored to the Church in these days. We ourselves may be 'unschooled' (4:13) or highly educated, but the only criteria for this ministry are 'faith in the name of Jesus' (3:16) and availability to the Holy Spirit, who alone can work such healing (and who takes no note of how much 'silver or gold' we have!).

If Peter had not responded to the prompting of the Spirit, the 40-year-old cripple would have lived out his days begging for survival. Furthermore, there would not have been such growth in the church (4:4). The public healing led to another opportunity for Peter to preach: miracles open people's hearts to hear God's message.

The authorities 'took note that [Peter and John] had been with Jesus' (4:13). Acts of kindness, prompted by the Spirit, will lead our friends and colleagues to note our allegiance to Jesus. As you reflect on these things, do you want to be open to the power of the Holy Spirit?

3 Fruit

Galatians 5:16–26

Paul's letter to the Galatian church is an eloquent apologetic for the truth that we are justified by faith. It was a response to the Judaisers, who were intent on including Jewish law in Christian practice. Paul's emphasis is on the Holy Spirit as central to the Christian life (v. 16). He uses the present continuous tense: 'go on living by the Spirit'. Daily we are to be led by the prompting and power of this gift of grace, rather than by trying to obey laws.

The Holy Spirit leads us away from sinful practice (vv. 19–21). Instead, the Christian is being transformed into the likeness of Jesus, to whom he or she belongs (v. 24). That likeness includes the 'fruit of the Spirit': love, joy, peace, patience, kindness, goodness, faithfulness, gentleness and self-control.

Some attributes are better caught than taught—and it is true that these fruits tend to 'rub off' on others. How important it is to be in regular fellowship with other Christians! We come together, perhaps after a week in a quite different climate, where such lovely qualities are absent. In an environment of Christian people, where the Holy Spirit reigns, there is encouragement for growth of a more truly human character, which glorifies God.

Notice that Paul says, 'Keep in step with the Spirit' (v. 25). We are to be a surrendered, led people: only with this attitude can we grow fruit. Think of a plant turning towards the sun, on which it depends.

Take some minutes to sit before God, turning yourself, as it were, towards the 'sun' of his face. Relax and read verses 22–23 slowly, reflecting on how each of those fruits would look in your own life and circumstances.

Try not to judge yourself if you find yourself lacking in these qualities. The Holy Spirit loves to grow them in us, so stay with the attitude of receiving from him. Ask God to help you to practise living in step with him daily.

4 Exercise

1 Corinthians 12

Michael Schluter, director of the Jubilee Centre in Cambridge, has reminded us that 'love… is not the language of finance or economics; it is the language of relationships. God measures a society… not by the size of its GNP or by the efficiency of its markets, but by the quality of its relationships' (*Cambridge Papers*, Vol. 6, No. 4, December 1997). This is the undergirding premise of New Testament teaching, based on the revealed love of God in Christ.

In 1 Corinthians 12, we read about the 'manifestation of the Spirit… given for the common good' (v. 7). Being open to the gifts of the Spirit is to be committed to living in loving relationship. It is a way of life in which we learn to live as part of 'the body', and as part of the world that God seeks to transform through his Church. Gifts are not, therefore, badges of status or signs of superiority.

Notice that it is the Holy Spirit who designs how the gifts are to be distributed (vv. 11, 18). He has a wonderful way of equipping believers with complementary gifts, and, when these gifts are being used together, the Church is a window on to God. As human beings we are easily led: are we 'led astray to mute idols' (v. 2), or are we seeking the leading and gifting of the Spirit?

Many of us approve gifts like teaching but are more vague about prophecy (vv. 10, 28). In fact, we have probably exercised the gift of prophecy without realising it. A prophetic word speaks life and encouragement into another's life; at times it may become a 'word of knowledge' (a message that goes beyond what someone could have known naturally). A way to develop this gift is to practise listening before praying for someone and allow ourselves to be led by God. He may give a specific sense of how to pray.

Another 'exercise' is to be open to the promptings of the Spirit during the day. Is someone on your mind? If so, send an email or make a phone call. Paul encourages us to 'eagerly desire' such gifts (v. 31), which will bless relationships and glorify God.

Take some time to ask God for his Spirit and to be open to his prompting. Then… exercise!

5 Community

Acts 2:42–47; 4:32–37

There is a poignant cry by the psalmist that each of us can hear echoing at times in our own experience: 'No one is concerned for me. I have no refuge; no one cares for my life' (Psalm 142:4). This cry of the human heart is for belonging, knowing connection with others and with God—the foundation of real living. Yet how many in our day still find themselves alone, unknown and disconnected?

The gift of the Holy Spirit heals these rifts, connecting us with the love of our Father and releasing us to live undefended lives with others. This is Church. 'Community' is a term used loosely today; true community is much more like the picture before us in these early chapters of Acts. Notice what is shared: meals, fellowship, possessions, homes, prayer, worship, teaching, helping the poor—this is not a neat and tidy lifestyle! The Spirit has broken down barriers, reserve and fear; in their place we read that the people enjoyed 'glad and sincere hearts' (2:46). As a reflection of the Trinity itself, God's people live in unity and self-offering relationships (4:32). It is in this context that God's power is manifest (2:43, 4:33).

You may recall that, before Pentecost, the disciples were behind locked doors for fear of the authorities (John 20:19). Many of us, too, have locked doors, which keep us from knowing the freedom of community and the power of God. Have we asked the Spirit of God to touch our lives? We can settle for less; it may be less risky. However, to experience the presence of God truly, we must relinquish our defences, our fears and our reserve and allow our lives to be interwoven with others', in service and in receiving. Only the Holy Spirit can effect this freedom.

In an attitude of receiving, ask God to fill you with his Spirit, giving permission for him to unlock your defences. Be still and rest with him. Then bring to mind those lives that intertwine with yours, giving thanks and holding before God the more challenging relationships. Does God want you to pray for one of these situations? Finally, pray for your church community, that the Spirit of gladness, transparency and power would bless you all.

6 Opposition

Acts 6:8–15; 7:51—8:1

The blood of Christian martyrs has been the foundation of countless revivals in the history of the Church. Here we read a detailed account of how the first martyr came to be falsely accused before his violent death.

How can it be that a man 'full of God's grace', who 'did great wonders' among the people, aroused opposition (6:8–9)? Stephen was teaching that the risen Jesus replaced the temple as the mediator of God's saving presence. The worship of God was no longer restricted to that place because disciples were praying through the Saviour. Those who guarded the temple tradition were unable to receive this freedom. They trumped up charges in order to defend their customs, rejecting not only Stephen but also the promised Messiah.

Notice that, as Stephen began his speech to the Sanhedrin, people 'saw that his face was like the face of an angel' (6:15). He was walking in the Spirit and, like his Master before him, became obedient to the point of death (see Philippians 2:8). When he challenged the rejection of Christ (7:51–53), the council were enraged; the contrast between Stephen's composure and forgiveness (v. 60) and the yelling and violence of the opposition is marked.

This death bore fruit because the believers were scattered across Judea and Samaria and the gospel was shared widely. In every generation, we carry the challenge to follow the Spirit, watching that we do not hold on to traditions that no longer serve the purposes of God. This account reminds us that to follow Jesus will bring opposition: he promised no less (John 15:20). Yet the Holy Spirit equipped Stephen to the end.

You may like to pray for your Christian community to be 'church' outside the walls, to sense the leading of the Spirit, and to be courageous and joyful even when facing opposition and misunderstanding.

Guidelines

I was struck by the courage of a gardening critic who expressed her disappointment with the Chelsea Flower Show! There was not enough beauty, she felt. The winning garden had no heart, no soul. It was cold. This seems to me to be a picture of our lives, too, without the warmth and beauty of the Holy Spirit. The promise of Jesus was that his coming would bring a 'full' life, in contrast to others, who may rob us of life or prove untrustworthy (John 10:10, 12).

Life to the full is a life exhibiting the fruit and gifts of the Spirit. It is a life lived in community, reaching out in the miraculous power of God, even risking conflict—all aspects of the Spirit's work that we have considered this week. The Holy Spirit enables this 'full' life to become reality in each of us: secured by the love of God, we are free to live. This is what Julian of Norwich said about such a life: 'Greatly should we rejoice that God dwells in our soul—and rejoice yet more because our soul dwells in God. Our soul is created to be God's home, and the soul is at home in the uncreated God' (*Revelations of Divine Love*).

You may like to spend a few minutes in quiet. Sometimes the love of God is received and known in this way. Allow yourself to be in Jesus' presence, resting in that security. Is there something he wants to say to you? Respond as a friend.

'May the grace of the Lord Jesus Christ, and the love of God, and the fellowship of the Holy Spirit be with you' (2 Corinthians 13:14).

Isaiah and the nations

Christians commonly view the prophecy of Isaiah as the high point of missionary theology in the Old Testament. Certainly, Isaiah is the Old Testament book with the most references to 'the nations'—that is, the Gentiles, those who are not members of the chosen people of God known as Israel. In our studies during the next fortnight we will explore the place of those nations within God's plan.

Isaiah is a complicated book. The eighth-century prophet whom God called (ch. 6) is the first named 'missionary' (*missio* means 'sending'). Isaiah was sent to his own people, a calling that not many would envy. During a prosperous period in the southern kingdom, he was to warn Judah and Jerusalem of their fate—spelling out the sin of the people, the desecration of the land and the prognosis of punishment. Though it doesn't yet look like it, exile is coming.

At first glance, this would hardly seem a promising start for an exploration of the place of 'the nations'. Yet Isaiah's oracles within the first main section of the book (Isaiah 1—39) relate to the nations over and over again. Many of them appear to address some of the nations surrounding Israel quite directly, and it turns out that Israel's own calling relates to the nations—not least in that Israel's current spiritual crisis will result in a political crisis, whereby the people of God will be carried off into 'the nations' as exiles in Babylon.

By chapter 40, Israel finds itself situated among the nations, where new questions arise as to the calling of God's people. Are they still God's people, even without their land, their king and their temple? What, then, is their calling?

Whereas chapters 1—39 are predominantly a message of judgment, chapters 40—66 present a message of comfort and hope. The first half of Isaiah addresses a people heading for exile; the second half meets the people in their exile, comforting them in their grief, yet challenging their self-pity. So the message is very different, as are the tone and style of writing. We move from prose to poetry. It is carefully composed and beautifully worded, as if to encourage the Israelites to memorise these words and allow them to ring in the heart over and over.

In reality, God's people need to learn afresh about their God. They need to relearn that he is the Creator of the universe, at a time when they doubt his power. They need reminding that he is not a creator who keeps a distance from his creation but a God who is deeply involved, grieving with those who mourn and getting his hands dirty for the sake of those he loves. They also need to rediscover who they are in God's purposes and receive his calling anew. Israel may have messed up and forgotten God, but God has not forgotten his people and they have not dropped out of his plan.

Quotations are taken from the New Revised Standard Version.

1 Guns to glory

Isaiah 2:1–4

The book of Isaiah opens with two visions, both 'concerning Judah and Jerusalem'. The first (ch. 1) concerns the present: the people's current state is one of sinfulness and hopelessness. The second concerns their future role in God's plan of salvation. This is a vision that could have been familiar, if the parallel text in Micah 4:1–3 was already known. It is possible, then, that God's people are being reminded of a role in God's plan that they have heard before. In any case, their present circumstances do not seem to dampen or disqualify their future prospects.

In fact, both Micah and Isaiah are reminding Israel of the big picture. The account of creation in Genesis 1 makes plain God's good intentions for the whole earth, not just for some people, and the call of Abraham in Genesis 12 brings into sharper focus God's plan of blessing for all people. The promised land and the chosen nation are established with a purpose— to convey God's blessing to every nation. Election is not for privilege but for service.

Isaiah 2 spells out how Israel should expect this to happen. Jerusalem is depicted at the centre of the world map, the focus of centrifugal forces that draw all nations in. Going 'up to the mountain of the Lord, to the house of the God of Jacob' (v. 3) suggests that these nations encounter YHWH in the way that God's chosen people Israel did at Sinai—by entering into covenant, observing the law and engaging in worship.

If so, this vision is radical. It is not clear whether Israel's role in the gathering of the nations is passive or active—whether the vision will be fulfilled reluctantly as the outcome of God's intentions alone or through the enthusiasm of God's people acting with evangelistic zeal. Certainly there are circumstances where the word of the Lord can and does 'go out' by itself, but it is usually enhanced by instruction and instructors.

Verse 4 spells out the extraordinary impact of this word: they shall not 'learn war any more'. The logical outcome of embracing God's covenant law is world peace. This peace is not the absence of difference: verse 4 assumes that it is still necessary for God to judge between nations. But it represents the constructive transformation of weaponry so as to disable the people for war and re-enable the land for fruitfulness.

2 Walking in the light

Isaiah 2:5–10

The glorious future vision of Isaiah 2:1–4 is not mere 'pie in the sky'. At least, the pie has implications at ground level and consequences for present realities. God's people—variously termed 'Israel' or the 'house of Jacob'—are urged to 'walk in the light of the Lord' (v. 5).

The principle is very simple. For God's people to lead others into God's paths, they themselves need to be walking in those paths. Unfortunately, they are not doing so: they have forsaken God's ways. Chapter 1 explained their sinfulness in terms of rebellion, corruption, estrangement, sickness, hypocrisy, futility, injustice and disobedience. Here the description of unfaithfulness is especially concrete: it relates to the adoption of alien religious practices, to the accumulation of wealth and weapons, and to the worship of idols.

What is the result? Verses 9–10 describe how the people will be humbled and humiliated—such that they will hide from God. The awesome glory of God is unwelcome and unwanted among a people who have chosen to worship their own gods. Indeed, God's glory is to be feared.

Who would resist the vision of global cooperation, harmony and peace described in the preceding vision? Those who fear that they stand to lose something. The vision describes the nations joining Israel on God's holy mountain. It does not discuss how this might affect Israel's special status as elect and chosen. It simply demands a willingness to set aside anything that is more precious—specifically the idols of wealth and weaponry, the usual means to material security—in order to focus entirely on the ways of God and to be transformed as they walk in his paths. Who is willing?

3 'The whole earth is full of his glory'… except Israel?

Isaiah 6:1–8

The prophet Isaiah is willing. We may imagine him in the temple, seeking God, at a time of national grief. The good king Uzziah has died, and his successor does not hold the same promise. Isaiah's prayer request, then, probably focused on his own nation's well-being.

His prayer is answered by a striking vision of none other than God himself. Even Moses, who communed with God 'face-to-face, as one speaks to a friend' (Exodus 33:11), was not allowed to see God (v. 20). Yet, just at the point when Isaiah is longing for a new human king in Judah, he glimpses God as the divine King, whose horizons stretch way beyond those of Judah.

Clearly Jerusalem is important to this King, for the hem of his robe touches down at this point on the planet. In the light of Jerusalem's importance, though, it's striking that God is presented as King of the universe, high above every nation, filling the whole earth with his glory. Is this a surprise? Not if we have taken on board God's original plan of universal blessing and his promise to Abraham in Genesis 12:3. But to any with a more parochial outlook—especially those who suppose themselves to be the unique locus of God's presence on earth—it may be surprising

To those who had embraced the message of judgment in the earlier chapters of Isaiah, there may be a further surprise. 'You mean, despite our sin, the hem of God's royal robe still touches us?' God's glory neither focuses purely on the chosen people nor resists the unfaithful people. In its transcendence it fills the whole earth without distinction; and in its immanence it reaches in to fill the temple—the particular place where sacrifice is made and forgiveness is sought.

This vision surely stretches Isaiah's horizons—to embrace God's awesome power and majesty over the universe, and yet to recognise God's forgiving grace to me, to us, here and now. The two are far from incompatible, according to God's ways.

The experience of this vision brings such profound enthusiasm for God that Isaiah volunteers to serve, like a school child with hand up, itching for the teacher to notice, yet not knowing to what or where. Isaiah models the response that is appropriate for all God's people.

It turns out that Isaiah's calling is less about the future promise of God (2:1–4) than the present predicament of God's people (vv. 5–10). I suspect that Isaiah would rather have been sent to a faraway nation as herald or teacher, yet he is called to disturb the comfortable close to home. Serving the God whose glory fills the whole earth may involve starting very locally and in just the place where that glory seems most scarce.

4 Judgment on Cush

Isaiah 18

You need a strong constitution to read the whole of Isaiah, not just the 'purple passages'. Chapter 18 is part of a long section (chs. 13—23) that is often skipped. The early chapters (1—12) focused on God's judgment of Judah and Jerusalem. Now we discover that the same arm of judgment is outstretched against the nations. One by one, each is named and addressed, forming an arc of those that are near and far in a full circle around Jerusalem. Because many of them, at various points during the eighth to sixth centuries BC, were enemies of Judah, this section of the prophecy would surely have been gratifying to its original audience. Imagine it: 'Phew, God doesn't like those Babylonians either!'

In chapter 18 the focus of God's fearful attention lands on Cush. This most probably relates to present-day Sudan, where the Dinka tribe in particular (among whom I have the privilege to visit and teach regularly) are indeed very tall and smooth-skinned. These people receive emissaries warning of a devastating attack, God's harsh reckoning at the time of judgment (vv. 5–6). The people of Cush, of Sudan, of Ethiopia, are to be laid waste, to become fodder for wild animals—just as was described in chapter 1, speaking of Judah and Jerusalem.

I chose this particular oracle of judgment from among the many because

I have read this text with some Sudanese Christians and listened with interest and surprise to their response. Where I expected fear or cynicism, I heard expressions of expectancy and grace. These people know first-hand about devastation and attack: their land has witnessed war for most of the past 50 years. The know that if the coming judgment is from God, then it will be just and fair—not racially and religiously motivated, as in recent experience. If judgment is the precursor to salvation, surely this act of God is to be welcomed: the pruning will be for good. Finally, the fact that these people are described and named in scripture, singled out among the nations, brings them honour ('You English are never mentioned,' one person said to me), even if they are singled out in the context of judgment.

This perspective is salutary. The time of reckoning is a time to be welcomed for those who have been on the underside of earthly injustice. Even oracles of judgment may be read as good news to the nations, for they confirm that God cares about them and includes them in his plan for justice and peace and salvation.

At that time, the 'Cushites' will bring gifts to Mount Zion (v. 7). Here is an echo of the vision of Isaiah 2. I suggest that we are invited to imagine the gifts as their tools of war, handed over so that they may become ploughshares and pruning hooks.

5 Judgment and salvation for Egypt

Isaiah 19:18–25

It is well worth reading the whole of chapter 19 if you have time. The Lord is riding on a 'swift cloud' that now alights in Egypt, where another oracle of judgment is delivered. The cloud has already travelled through Babylon, Assyria, Philistia, Moab, Damascus and Cush. Now it falls on Israel's arch-enemy of old, rehearsing and reversing some of the problems Israel experienced during its slavery—idols, a fierce taskmaster as ruler, and drought. Imagine the relish with which the Israelites must have rubbed their hands at verse 17: 'And the land of Judah will become a terror to the Egyptians…'.

Yet the tide turns suddenly in this chapter. 'On that day' denotes not just the day of harsh judgment but also a day of transformation when 'five cities in the land of Egypt' will 'swear allegiance to the Lord of hosts'

(v. 18). Do you feel the shock waves? Here is a statement about Israel's enemies, their former slave-drivers, turning to Israel's God! Moreover, this allegiance is not reluctant: the people will worship him and cry to him in their oppression, and 'he will send them a saviour, and will defend and deliver them' (v. 20). Does this sound familiar? Here is the language used to describe the Israelite slaves in Egypt and their exodus, the defining event of salvation according to the Hebrew Bible—now applied to *the Egyptians* in their oppression. At this point we may imagine shock turning to horror among Isaiah's audience. How could God be so merciful? Doesn't God shun those who shun his people? The answer is that God strikes Egypt and heals Egypt. Judgment and salvation are opposite sides of the same coin.

The text continues to surprise and horrify Israelite ears. Verse 23 describes a highway between Egypt and Assyria, the two powers that represented the greatest threat to Israel in the eighth century. Whereas previously the highway enabled the exodus of Israel out of Egypt, and even out of Assyria (11:16), here is a reverse exodus—we may presume, for the salvation of Egyptians and Assyrians. Finally, when Israel is named and affirmed as a blessing in the midst of the earth, it is as 'the *third*' people. The gold and silver medals will go to Egypt and Assyria. The people of God are being prepared to share the podium of honour, salvation and blessing, for the God of Israel is also, clearly, the God of Egypt and of Assyria. Everything that God has invested in Israel as 'my people' is also destined for others.

6 Judgment and restoration

Isaiah 34 and 35

After the oracles against the nations (chs. 13—23), the first major section of the book of Isaiah offers a mini 'apocalypse' (chs. 24—27) followed by some more historically focused passages warning Judah and Jerusalem of their condition and fate. Then comes this chapter-pair that functions as a summary for all of First Isaiah. Here we find a chapter describing God's terrible universal judgment, followed by a chapter anticipating a joyful homecoming in which all creation is restored.

I would guess that chapter 35 is familiar to readers, and that chapter 34 is not. Of course, we love to skip to passages that we find encouraging and hopeful, even at the expense of misappropriating that hope. Israel made the same mistake. But these two chapters form a little *inclusio* describing God's fearsome work of judgment followed by the joyful work of renewal. The two belong together.

Note how chapter 34 begins by addressing all nations, all peoples, the earth, the world. Even though, from verse 5, the particular nation of Edom comes into focus, it is understood that what God is doing in Edom will take place universally. It is all 'doomed' (v. 2): all that is in defiance of God is destined for destruction.

Yet destruction is not the end. God's work of judgment is the essential preparation for his promised work of renewal, recovery and redemption. Although chapter 35 has been classically understood to anticipate Israel's return to Jerusalem after the exile, the return is much more far-reaching: the description is of the re-creation of the whole created order. It is universal: the highway for God's people (v. 8) has relevance far beyond the historically defined Old Testament Israelite people of God, as does the reference to the redeemed and the ransomed (vv. 9–10). The historical experience of exile and return will offer a worked example—a small-scale means of appropriating God's promises—of the mind-boggling implications of God's planned new creation.

Guidelines

The first section of Isaiah emphasises God as 'the Holy One of Israel', who has a plan, an unshakeable plan, for Israel and for the nations. Sometimes it is hard to follow: certainly we may imagine the people of God alternating between confusion and complacency. But what is underlined here is the way in which the people of God are invited to participate within it, as those already invested with a covenant relationship, and so to help bring it about.

The plan encompasses judgment and salvation, for Israel and for all the nations. Neither triumphalism nor despair are appropriate, only an awareness of God as 'the Holy One of Israel'. That title spells out God's particular commitment to a particular people, yet it also emphasises the key quality of God's character—holiness—according to which he cannot be contained.

1 'Here is your God!'

Isaiah 40:1–11

These words—known and loved so well, thanks to Handel's *Messiah*—represent the dulcet tones of a lover, wooing his beloved with a song from the heart. God's people are fragile, bearing a sense of both political and personal abandonment owing to the experience of exile. But God has not abandoned them, at least not for long: here he comforts them, releases them and prepares them.

For what is he preparing them? A highway is promised (v. 3), reminiscent of that which led the Israelites out of slavery—but this highway is for God, the God who is coming. God gets the red carpet treatment, like visiting royalty. Is he coming back to Israel to reclaim his errant people? Much more than that: 'Then the glory of the Lord shall be revealed, and *all people* shall see it together' (v. 5, emphasis mine).

Exactly what Isaiah was privileged to glimpse in chapter 6 is now promised, not just to Israel but to all people. Isaiah glimpsed the glory and holiness of God, high and lofty, sitting on a throne and filling the earth. Now, it is foretold, all flesh shall see what Isaiah saw.

As in chapter 6, this vision also constitutes a call. The people, though they are as frail as grass, are called to shout the good news from the mountain top. They are to be the heralds, the evangelists, those who prepare the way for God's royal arrival. This announcement, then—though often received historically as a message of good news to Israel, promising the end of exile in Babylon—is actually the announcement of a universal arrival, impacting all people everywhere. For Israel, the good news is that they are receiving a renewed invitation to be involved in God's plans, to offer themselves for faithful service in the manner of Isaiah. They are to prepare the way and announce the news so that all people will be ready for the glory of God—and, by the grace of God, in the process, they will find themselves included as recipients of salvation also.

The message of this text for the Church is little different from its message for Israel. The good news of salvation is not something that God announces to the Church. It is something that God announces to the world, *through* the Church.

2   Is your God this big?

After the grand announcement and invitation comes a piece of creation theology in the form of a poem addressing the depth of God's wisdom and the extent of God's action. These words are intended (in the words of Hilaire Belloc) 'to make one gasp and stretch one's eyes' to the magnitude of God's creativity.

The poem proceeds by way of a series of rhetorical questions inviting speculation on God's greatness (and, by comparison, on human finitude). Who has measured the waters… weighed the mountains? Who was God's teacher? To whom will you liken God? Do you not know? Have you not understood? Who created these? Why do you speak? These questions are answered by assertions and images designed to boggle the mind concerning God, before whom 'the nations are like a drop from a bucket… the isles like fine dust… [the earth's] inhabitants are like grasshoppers' (vv. 15, 22).

If you have lost your home, a refugee living against your will in a foreign land, it is likely that you might feel like dust blown in a careless wind, or like a grasshopper trodden down by unfriendly feet. This chapter attempts to help us journey beyond our sense of our world to recognise God's sense of God's world. The perspective is very different.

It is hard not to think of ourselves at the centre of the world—if only because we learn our concepts of the world from the things around us. At a mission-minded church service recently, the pastor led the congregation to pray 'for strangers in remote parts of the world'—a statement that distracted me to wonder to whom such people were strange or remote. Certainly not to God, I suspect!

Moreover, when times are tough, our world is prone to get smaller: we instinctively curl up to resist further pain or pressure. This describes the condition of Israel in exile. To such situations, this poem comes not only as inspiration but as challenge. God has not forgotten them or abandoned them; moreover, the Creator of the universe is not anxious or flustered. He who 'also' created the stars, who calls each one by name, can handle this little hiccup. Those who worry that they have fallen out of the plan need to be reminded that it is *God's* plan, not theirs. It is not only about them, even though, by God's gracious invitation again and again, it can and will and does include them. God's plan is about God—the God who holds the whole universe in the gentle, steady palm of his hand.

3 Justice in the earth, light to the nations

Isaiah 42:1–9

The first of the so-called 'servant songs' resounds with the clearest message about the nations. God's servant is tasked with establishing justice in the earth (v. 4), being given as a covenant to the people and a light to the nations (v. 6).

As anyone who has tried to establish justice between unhappy siblings (let alone warring nations) will know, this is a costly call. It is no simple listening process: the servant is implicated as a covenant, somehow embodying the reconciliation and light that he brings. Clearly the servant has reason to cry in weakness and even break down from pain (vv. 2–3), but he does not grow faint and is not crushed. The same power that was promised in 40:28–31, for the strengthening of the powerless and the renewal of the weary, is promised again here, explained by the assurance, 'I have put my spirit upon him' (v. 1).

The spirit that is promised is (as in chapter 40) closely related to the God of creation (v. 5). Thus the calling and the strength to fulfil the calling are given in the context of God's creation of the earth. On reflection, the logic seems obvious: that which God creates, God redeems; and those whom God calls, God equips.

The biggest remaining question is one that has vexed readers and scholars for centuries, and over which Jews and Christians commonly divide: who is the servant? To whom does this calling refer? We have insufficient space to do justice to the complexity of the issues related to this question, given that almost every significant figure in the Old Testament (from Adam to Moses to David to Hezekiah to Cyrus), as well as (of course) Jesus, are regularly named. Here I simply want to point out the answer that presents itself within the frame of the immediate context of Isaiah.

The most obvious answer to the question 'Who is the servant?' is 'Israel'. The title of 'servant' is regularly used for the collective body of God's people: it has been applied to Israel repeatedly in the previous chapter (see 41:8–9). If chapters 40—41 served a forlorn and downtrodden people with a reaffirmation of their identity and place in God's plan, then this text from chapter 42 reminds them what it means, and what it costs. Their calling as God's covenant people is to *be* a covenant to all peoples and nations. It may be costly but it will be rewarding (v. 7). In the end, it is the ultimate calling—and it may be the only calling (vv. 8–9).

4 There is no other

Isaiah 45:1–7

What, then, are we to make of God's calling to Cyrus—a foreigner, the king of Persia?

The familiar language used to describe this alien ruler is redolent with terms normally confined to Israel as God's holy people, belonging to the context of commitment and covenant. God speaks 'thus' to Cyrus, in just the manner that he speaks to his own people and prophets. God promises to go before Cyrus in protection and preparation. He calls Cyrus by name as he called Israel by name—echoing and, arguably, fulfilling the promises delivered to Israel in chapter 41. Even more significant is the description of Cyrus as 'his anointed' (v. 1): the Hebrew has the same root as 'messiah', suggesting some surprising fulfilment of the messianic promises found earlier in Isaiah (chs. 9 and 11).

On the one hand, God appears to be functioning on intimate terms with a person who is not of God's people. On the other, God is acting 'for the sake of my servant Jacob, and Israel my chosen' (v. 4). God is doing something surprising, shocking, even scandalous—something that could be regarded as betrayal—yet he is doing it out of devotion towards his beloved people.

It seems that God can and does call anyone, but his choice and calling are meant to fulfil the purposes and plans that have been declared over and over again. These plans and purposes centre on Israel historically but are not exclusive to Israel theologically. Thus a foreign king can not only come to know the Lord (v. 3) but can serve him also, even without realising it (v. 4).

Exploring the theme of 'Israel and the nations' in Isaiah throws us back to exploring more about the Lord, the God who created every nation and called Israel to be his holy nation. If there is no other God (v. 6), it follows logically that God is responsible for light and darkness, weal and woe, conquering enemies and unknown friends. Israel in exile appears to be charged with relearning this logic. If the God of Israel is the only God, then (at least) two conclusions follow. First, the Israelites are to serve him because there is nowhere else to go; and second, the God of Israel may have claims on (and plans for) people well beyond Israel. If so, then we might expect to find God calling 'aliens' into his service—surprising people fulfilling strategic roles in precisely those areas where the more predictable suspects have failed.

Here in the middle of Second Isaiah, God's dealings with some non-Israelites prove deeply challenging, while becoming a saving grace, for the Israelite people of God. Cyrus turns out to be God's instrument for rescuing the Israelites from exile and returning them to their own land. God's grace is conveyed through alien hands, even where such strangers do not recognise their role in mediating God's grace or God's plan.

5 God's holy mountain

Isaiah 56:1–8

What, then, is Israel to do with strangers who choose to serve the God of Israel? On what terms are they welcome? Chapter 56—commonly thought to introduce the third and final section of the book of Isaiah, addressing itself to the post-exilic situation after the people of Israel have returned to their homeland—describes a situation in which foreigners are 'joined to the Lord'.

Such foreigners are those who are not Israelites/Jews through biological descent, yet have become associated with the Israelites through religious observance. The text implies that the covenant between God and Israel is now extended to all who are faithful. All who maintain justice and do righteousness (v. 1, in contrast to the Israelites before exile; see 5:16–23), who keep sabbath, resist evil and seek to please God, are given an everlasting name. No longer is race or circumcision the key—only faithfulness to the covenant.

It is not just that these 'outsiders' may become as 'insiders'. Verse 6 describes them as ministering to the Lord as God's *servants*. In the context of the book of Isaiah, where the term 'servant' has received such emphasis, here is another startling statement about Gentiles—as startling as describing a foreign king as 'anointed' (45:1). In 42:1–8, the role of servant was described in terms of reaching out to the coastlands and being a light to the Gentiles, reaffirming Israel's original call. As the servant passages in Second Isaiah gather momentum (in particular at 49:1–7; 50:4–9; 52:13—53:12), the servant figure is increasingly set over against Israel and, through his suffering, brings about vindication for all, not just for Israel. Thus may we Christians legitimately identify the servant as Jesus, even as we also recognise that, originally, Israel was called to be the servant.

So we may suggest that Cyrus is the forerunner for countless Gentile servants of the Lord, those who help to bring about God's promises. Through church ministry I have learned the truth of the dictum 'Use them or lose them'. In God's kingdom, it is clear that God uses all comers.

Where do they come to? Notice the reference to God's holy mountain (v. 7), a deliberate echo of chapter 2. In the eighth-century context of Judah's prosperity and blindness, this image came as a revisioning of Israel's larger purpose and role in God's overarching future plan. Here, after the lessons of the exile, it seems that the future is breaking in. At last there would seem to be a 'normal' expectation of foreigners in Jerusalem—even if they are still labelled 'foreigners'!

6 The role of the servant

Isaiah 61:1–7

Our final passage in this series is sometimes called 'the fifth servant song', and comes as both summary and challenge. It brings together the royal imagery of anointing, associated with the messianic promises of a future Davidic ruler inaugurating a reign of peace (chs. 9; 11), with the role of the servant to bring about justice on earth, accompanied by and achieved through vicarious suffering.

This text is often referred to as 'the Nazareth manifesto' because Jesus read from this chapter in the synagogue at Nazareth and then declared, 'Today this scripture has been fulfilled in your hearing' (Luke 4:21). We are used to recognising the multiple ways in which Jesus represents and completes this picture—not least as both suffering servant and Messiah.

Yet the question remains: whom was the passage understood to address when it was first delivered? I suggest, once again, that all Israel, the people of God, are intended to take on the mantle of the servant. Here is Isaiah's answer to the vision set out in chapter 2, where all nations stream to the holy mountain to learn God's ways. Now, unlike the situation in Jerusalem described then, God's people are displaying God's glory (v. 3), building up the city (v. 4) and functioning as priests and ministers (v. 6). In the light of chapter 56, we might imagine that God's people also include those who have been incorporated from other nations.

As well as offering a fitting conclusion, this passage presents a challenge. Despite the suggestion in Isaiah 56 that proselytes might become integrated within Israel, here we find 'strangers' and 'foreigners' described in subservient roles, with suggestions that Israel is luxuriating in the wealth of the nations. The overtones of 'apartheid'—of some form of slavery or racism—are hard to miss. History would suggest that privilege is rarely given up or shared easily.

It seems clear that some tension exists concerning the place of the nations in God's holy city. Is it that strangers were welcomed as friends before the complications of integration were fully acknowledged—and resisted? Is it that the earlier vision offers a rhetoric to aim for, and that this chapter more closely describes the reality? Either way, chapter 61, exuberant and exhilarating as it is in terms of the good news and its impact, challenges any naïve 'missionary theology' that we might seek in Isaiah. Jerusalem functions at the centre of the map. 'Strangers' are welcomed, but they may remain just that—strangers. This is hardly the picture found in Revelation, where all are equal around God's throne—not singled out by race or nationality or tongue, despite a recognition of diversity. Nor is it the way in which Jesus took up the servant role during his earthly ministry.

Guidelines

The message of Isaiah delivers good news to the oppressed, liberty to captives and comfort for all who mourn. That good news is not simply a message to Israel but a message for Israel to bring to the world.

In the person of Jesus we see God (Isaiah 40). We also recognise in Jesus God's chosen servant, perfectly fulfilling Israel's call—not just in word but in deed; not just to Israel but to Gentiles; not just in life but in death. By taking on the role of the vicariously suffering servant, Jesus becomes the covenant to the people, the light to the nations and the means of bringing justice to the ends of the earth.

Just as the Israelites were called to mission as servants, so are we as Christians. We cannot rest content to say, 'Jesus did that.' Our calling is to walk in Jesus' footsteps. God's plans operate like a relay race, and we are those to whom the baton has now been passed.

God's holy mountain is now understood more spiritually than geographically (see John 4 for the way in which Jesus reinterprets the tradition for a Samaritan). Nevertheless, God's plan continues for the ingathering of all nations and for peace around the throne of grace. There, the God whom Isaiah was privileged to glimpse as king, high and lofty, will be enthroned above all people—the same God that we have come to know in the servant who suffered.

FURTHER READING

John Goldingay, *Isaiah* (New International Biblical Commentary), Hendrickson, 2001.

Jo Bailey Wells, *Isaiah* (The People's Bible Commentary), BRF, 2006.

Chris Wright, *The Mission of God: Unlocking the Bible's Grand Narrative*, IVP Academic, 2006.

Luke 7—10

We continue our study of Luke's Gospel, begun two issues ago. In those previous studies we have seen that Luke was written for those who already knew the story of Jesus, but aimed to reveal more clearly the truth of those events, including the inner truth of how God was fulfilling his purposes through them. The 'infancy narratives' highlighted three themes (expectations, obedience and reversal) and we saw these continue to be developed in chapters 3—6. Jesus defied expectations by his manifesto of reversal—the rich being sent empty away and the good news being preached to the poor and marginal. Indeed, as the story unfolded we saw how far this reversal went—Jesus offering welcome and forgiveness to the wicked. Alongside this there was demonstration of Jesus' power in word and action, and the call to others to follow him—to be obedient and responsive—and, indeed, as children of God, to imitate God.

Over the next three weeks we will continue to explore these themes. In particular, the distinctiveness of Jesus is highlighted: his message and status are fundamentally different from those of contemporary religious figures. We also hear of the importance and challenge of response—a threefold response—to Jesus' teaching, to Jesus himself and to God. Are we prepared to walk the road of discipleship?

Unless otherwise stated, quotations are taken from the NRSV.

14–20 June

1 A centurion's slave

Luke 7:1–10

At his birth Jesus was proclaimed as 'a light for revelation to the Gentiles and for glory to your people Israel' (2:32). This account reminds us of that promise and challenges any stereotypical view that the Jewish religious authorities were opposed to Jesus, and anti-Gentile. Here we see a more hopeful strand of life within Israel.

The centurion would have been an important figure in the occupying army, so we might expect Israel's leaders to shun him. In fact, though, he seems to have a strong, positive relationship with them. Not only do the elders plead with Jesus to help him, but the centurion himself shows sensitivity to Jewish customs by urging Jesus not to come into his house (thus avoiding ritual 'pollution'). Here is a senior Roman soldier exemplifying how the differences between Gentile and Jew need not result in violence and hatred.

Jesus' words 'I have not found such great faith even in Israel' (v. 9, NIV) need not have any negative implication. The centurion's faith is testimony to the amazing greatness of God's mercy; it need not be an implicit criticism of Israel. The centurion and the Jewish elders who support him are all examples of the good tree producing good fruit and the wise man who built his house upon rock (Luke 6:43, 48). Matthew 8:5–13, however, tells a similar story with a negative slant. In Matthew's story there are no supportive Jewish elders; Jesus' commendation of the centurion's faith is a criticism of Israel, and he concludes with a declaration that some in Israel will be excluded from the kingdom.

Matthew's version fits with our natural tendency to stereotype, perhaps expecting oppressive Roman soldiers and inward-looking Jewish religious authorities. Those of us who are Gentile Christians may not even find the Gentile centurion's faith surprising, for it fits our understanding that Jesus' own people did not accept him (John 1:11) and that it was Gentiles like us who trusted in Jesus. In our prejudices, it is actually the positivity of the Jewish elders and the lack of Jew–Gentile tension in Luke that surprises us.

Jesus found goodness and faith—good trees producing good fruit—in all kinds of people, of different backgrounds, races, occupations and even religions, and they in turn responded to him. Do we need to open our eyes to see signs of the kingdom in unexpected places?

2 A widow's son

Luke 7:11–17

This event not only happens 'soon after' the previous one (v. 11) but fits well with it thematically. There are various points of connection, starting with the fact that it is another miraculous healing. The widow is one of the marginalised or weak in society (particularly now that her son has died);

and the same, in a different way, could be said of the centurion: he was on the edge of Jewish society.

There are also important differences. Here Jesus acts completely on his own initiative: nobody asks for his help; there is no mention of faith. Here he deliberately touches the coffin, incurring corpse uncleanliness—one of the most clearly defined forms of ritual pollution—whereas the centurion actively avoided any such pollution. Also, God's care for widows is a recurring theme throughout the Old Testament (for example, Psalm 68:5). This is perhaps reflected in the positive news about Jesus that spread after this miracle (vv. 16–17): prophets were meant to help widows.

Two points arise from this passage and the previous one. First, we are reminded that Jesus is 'the saviour' of the Jewish people (2:11). He is acting in keeping with the great prophets of old (particularly Elijah in 1 Kings 17:8–24 and Elisha in 2 Kings 4:8–36). There is much continuity in Jesus' ministry with the Old Testament and Jewish hopes. He is the Jewish Messiah, whose blessing also overflows to Gentiles. As the previous story showed, this need not be divisive. It is a straightforward truth that 'God has looked favourably on his people' (Luke 7:16). Together the stories show the breadth of Jesus' mission. Second, the contrasts challenge any idea that there is a set of rules by which God acts. Faith is important in one story but absent in the other. Compassion features in one, not the other. In different ways, those healed might be classed as insiders or outsiders, weak or powerful, traditionally pious or marginal.

It is perhaps only human to try to create a set of rules that God's actions must follow, but it is good to be reminded of how foolish this is. If we are to act with and for God in our world, it will not be because we have worked out God's rules but because God has opened our eyes to see people as he does, and because we have started to grasp his compassion for all.

3 Expectations and fulfilment

Luke 7:18–28

We return to the theme of the continuity and discontinuity between Jesus and Jewish expectations. John's question is a natural response to the miracles that Luke has just recounted. Jesus appears to be acting like one of the former prophets, bringing favour to his people (7:16–17) and showing that God's mercy is not confined to Israel (a point that seems to have been important to John: see 3:8). John had seen his role as preparing for the 'coming one' (3:16) so it is not surprising that he wonders about Jesus. Indeed, Luke deliberately points out to us that Jesus' actions fulfil Old Testament prophecies (compare verse 22 with Isaiah 35:5–6).

Nevertheless there is still a discontinuity between John's expectations and Jesus' actions, which perhaps explains John's lack of certainty (v. 20). John had spoken of the coming one bringing wrath and judgment (3:7, 17), and John's role was to prepare the people by encouraging repentance (1:17, quoting Malachi 4:6). Jesus, however, is showing mercy and forgiveness, not bringing judgment, so is he really the coming one?

This highlights the importance of Jesus' words, 'Blessed is anyone who takes no offence at me' (v. 23), for in them we see a negative side to Jesus' mission. As Simeon said (2:34), he will cause the *falling* as well as the rising of many. Some will find his actions unacceptable, refusing to acknowledge that he is truly the agent of God, and in that way will face judgment. Jesus transforms expectations by his focus on mercy and forgiveness, and yet fulfils them because, through him, judgment does come.

Jesus' words about John (vv. 24–28) further emphasise Jesus' claim to be 'the coming one'. John is the 'messenger' of Malachi 3:1; therefore Jesus is the one being prepared for. He then manages to praise John (thus further confirming that John's message about a 'coming one' is true) and yet at the same time put a great gulf between John and the kingdom of heaven that Jesus is announcing. Jesus is heralding something new. Judgment is still there—the demand for justice remains—but the overwhelming message is one of grace and salvation. It's a challenge in our lives, as disciples and as churches, to manifest this gospel and not fall back into the message of John.

4 Jesus and John

Luke 7:29–35

The relationship between Jesus and John is important. John prepared the people for Jesus: it was those whom John had baptised who responded positively to Jesus (vv. 29–30) and Jesus himself started within John's movement. (Jesus was baptised by John and some of Jesus' disciples were originally John's.) Despite this, however, they were very different people.

Two points arise from Jesus' words (vv. 31–35). First, whatever God's messengers do—whether they are like John or like Jesus—many people will reject them. John was 'too holy'—the fanatic or fundamentalist, separated from the normal things of life. Jesus was 'not holy enough'. We can often think 'If only we get the medium correct, if only we communicate in the right way, then people will understand.' Of course, it is important to think seriously about how to communicate the gospel in particular cultures and communities. However, Jesus' words remind us that even with multiple different approaches, people can still be resistant. People may complain that church is boring but, if you take them to a livelier one, they complain that it is too noisy or there is no quiet space for prayer. Both can be God's will: 'wisdom is proved right by *all* her children' together (v. 35, NIV). Presumably John and Jesus were different because they had different roles in God's plan. This also reminds us that we should be open-hearted to those who manifest their devotion to God in ways very different from our own.

Second, it is worth pondering the description given of Jesus in verse 34. He is not the archetypal 'holy man'. Indeed, he is positively nothing like that—that was what John was like, and it was obvious to everyone that Jesus was very different. I would love to see a depiction of this passage with Jesus and John standing next to each other. In my imagination, John would look like the holy man, determined and gaunt from a life of hardship in the desert. Jesus would perhaps be a little overweight, softer, with a pallor from going to too many parties. Most of us find that a disturbing idea, but why? What implicit ideas of holiness do we have? Often, they are life-denying, connecting godliness with hardship, 'denying the flesh' and rejection of the pleasures of life. Many of Jesus' contemporaries had the same ideas, and hence rejected Jesus.

5 Love and forgiveness

Luke 7:36–50

This beautiful story continues the exploration of the distinctiveness of Jesus' message and his relationship with other religious figures around him. First note that Jesus is depicted as being on good terms with Simon, the Pharisee. Although elsewhere we find Jesus and the Pharisees at odds with each other, here we are reminded that many Pharisees would have recognised Jesus as a fellow interpreter of the law, calling the people back to God. Nor is it fair to suggest that Jesus is critical of Simon in the passage: Jesus is not really complaining that Simon did not give him any water, kisses or oil (vv. 44–45); he is just pointing out how extraordinary the woman's actions are. Jesus speaks kindly to him—'Simon, I have something to tell you' (v. 40, NIV)—Simon responds respectfully, and in the end Jesus implies that Simon himself has been forgiven, even if only a little were needed (v. 47).

However, there is a gulf between Jesus and Simon, revealed in verse 39. Simon automatically assumes that if Jesus knew what sort of woman was touching him, he would reject her adoration (the description of her suggests that she was a prostitute). The fact that Jesus does not reject her suggests to Simon that Jesus cannot be quite the prophet that his public reputation suggests. But Simon is wrong. Jesus does know all about the woman but his attitude towards 'sinners' is fundamentally different from that of Pharisees such as Simon, and he cares little for appearances or ideas of pollution.

The point of Jesus' story is obvious but also quite profound. Both people in the story have received the same treatment. They have both been forgiven. Thus, the implication is that both the righteous (like Simon) and the sinful will be treated the same by God. God does not favour Pharisees such as Simon, but nor does God favour sinners and outcasts: they both receive forgiveness. However, it is hardly surprising if the outcasts and sinners are more overjoyed at receiving God's favour than the righteous. It is as if Jesus is trying to help Simon understand that sinners who find forgiveness may, out of their overwhelming joy, react in ways that seem 'out of place'.

Jesus' message seems lost on the other guests. They are unable to grasp the story of love, acceptance and joy played out in front of them. All they can see is a theological argument about who can forgive sins (v. 49). It is all too easy to bury Jesus' message of joy, love and transformation under a heavy weight of theology, expectations and respectability.

6 The parable of the soil

Luke 8:1–15

This is not the parable of the sower but the parable of the soil. The same seed is scattered widely by the same sower, in a seemingly indiscriminate and wasteful process (just as Jesus' itinerant ministry, speaking in villages and fields, might have seemed indiscriminate). What makes the difference is the soil. The parable is about the different responses that different people make to God's word, to Jesus' proclamation of the kingdom. Some do not really hear; some respond with joy but soon forget it; some make a proper start but still do not produce; some, with a 'honest and good heart' (v. 15), respond properly. This makes sense of Jesus' exhortation in verse 8: if you are capable of responding, then respond, for what makes the difference is not the seed (which goes everywhere) but the welcome it receives.

The dialogue in verses 9–10 (quoting Isaiah 6:9) takes the point further. When asked about this parable, Jesus' response is about parables in general: the parable of the soil is actually a parable about parables. The purpose of all the parables is to call for a response. Everyone hears the parables (everyone is 'seeing' and 'hearing') but some will not respond (many 'may not see [or] understand'). This parable about parables tells us that understanding a parable and responding to it are synonymous. If you do not understand, you will not respond. If you have not responded, you have not really understood. (If the corn does not grow, the seed has not properly taken root.)

In verse 10 Jesus says that his followers have been given the secret of understanding. But in the previous chapters we see that Jesus' followers are not special in any way save one: they have responded to Jesus. Finally the point becomes clear. Everyone hears the parables but they are only actually understood by those who respond positively to them, take them in and act upon them—and that cannot be done separately from responding positively to Jesus, taking him in and acting on what he says. The people's response to the word being preached is the other side of the same coin of their response to Jesus the preacher. Knowledge cannot be separated from commitment; the 'message of Christianity' cannot be separated from Jesus. The women (vv. 2–3) had responded, both in their lives and with their money. They are examples of those who 'hold it fast in an honest and good heart, and bear fruit with patient endurance' (v. 15).

Guidelines

Five key aspects of the gospel message have emerged in this week's readings:

- Jesus is for all people, equally.
- Jesus' desire is to bring mercy and forgiveness.
- Jesus does bring division, as people either respond or do not respond to him.
- You cannot separate the man from the message: responding to Jesus and understanding his teaching are two sides of the same coin.
- Responding to Jesus is personal and life-changing, a matter of the heart.

Perhaps there is one of these observations that makes you feel uneasy, or has struck you afresh. It may be worth pondering further. Does the church you are part of seem to overlook or hide any of these aspects? What difference does that make? What could be done about it?

1 Response is everything

Luke 8:16–21

The theme of the parable of the soil is continued in these passages. Jesus highlights that there is no secret teaching to be transmitted to an inner group. Just as light is not hidden, so his preaching is public and open: anything that might have seemed hidden in God's plan will be revealed. However, once again the issue is 'how you listen'. The light on the stand only illuminates 'those who enter' (v. 16). This is also the meaning of verse 18. This is not about money—as if God blesses with more money those who already have it, and takes away from those who are destitute. On the contrary, it is again about response. Those who have understood/responded to Jesus will gain further understanding by their response. Those who do not respond will lose even the small amount of understanding that they had. Verse 17 perhaps also implies judgment: how we respond will not be for ever a private matter. In the end it will be revealed, just as, in the parable of the soil, the way the ground has received the seed is finally demonstrated by the lack or presence of a crop.

Everything hinges on response. Even those closest to Jesus—his mother and brothers—have no particular call on him or understanding of him merely as a result of their family relationship (v. 21). What matters for his biological family, and for everyone else, is their response to the word of God and how they put it into practice—as was said of the wise and foolish builders in 6:46–49. Notice again that in 6:46–49 it was Jesus' words that required a response; here is it God's word. The two are clearly equivalent: as Jesus preaches God's word, responding to Jesus' words is the same as responding to God's word. Furthermore, as we saw in the explanation of the parable of the soil (8:9–15), responding to God's word is the same as responding to Jesus himself.

This focus on response puts the responsibility on to us. If there was some secret teaching, hidden from most of us, then most of us would have an excuse for being half-hearted at best in following Jesus. But there isn't. It's all revealed; nobody has any special favours or insight. What matters is whether we 'pay attention to how we listen' (v. 18). Do we 'hear the word of God and do it?' Or do we collude with the idea that there is some 'secret teaching' or 'hidden insight' to let ourselves off the hook?

2 Jesus calms the storm

Luke 8:22–25

Luke's narrative now moves on to a sequence of miracle stories. The section starts with the extremely vague 'one day' (v. 22) but then flows all the way through to verse 56. This must have been an extremely memorable day! The chronological relationship between this day and the teaching earlier in the chapter is far less important; indeed, Jesus may well have repeated similar teaching on different occasions.

The story itself is straightforward, demonstrating that Jesus has authority not only over sickness and demons affecting individuals but over nature far more broadly. In the Old Testament, control over the sea is seen as a revelation of the enormity of God's power (see Psalm 89:9; 106:9). Thus, Jesus is displaying power associated only with God. Note also that the disciples respond with fear (v. 25)—the classic response to a demonstration of divine power.

The story highlights two areas for reflection. First, we should take seriously the structure of the passage, with its climax as the disciples' question, 'Who is this?' The purpose of this miracle is to point towards Jesus' identity. We are not allowed to ask just 'Do I like his teaching?' We must ask, 'Who is this person?' The previous passages have shown that these questions are closely related: our response to Jesus is the other side of the same coin as our response to his teaching/the word of God. Even so, the question 'Who is he?' is more uncomfortable. Assessing teaching leaves us in control: we can like one aspect, tone down another and harmonise a third with teaching from elsewhere. But 'Who is this?' forces questions of loyalty and commitment, for the disciples and for us.

Second, we note that the disciples are criticised for their lack of faith. They should have known better. This is the first occurrence in Luke of a theme that will recur with greater frequency toward the end of the Gospel. The disciples do not seem to have the trust in, understanding of and loyalty towards Jesus that their position might suggest, and that Jesus seems to hope for. How satisfactory is their response to him? Are they perhaps like the seed sown among the thorns—starting well but ultimately failing? Many of us like to echo the words of the father in Mark 9:24 ('I believe; help my unbelief'—interestingly, not recorded in the equivalent, Luke 9:37–43). Here, though, we have to face the disciples, and perhaps ourselves, being criticised for our lack of faith. It seems that we are, at least in part, responsible for how much faith we have. Are we committed to developing it?

3 Overthrowing the Legion

Luke 8:26–39

This incident demonstrates Jesus' power in another area. So far in the chapter we have seen power in teaching, then over nature and now over demons. Once again, though, the issue it leaves us with (vv. 34–39) is response.

The story is rich with detail. The region of the Gerasenes was a predominantly Gentile area (note the pigs). However, Luke does not emphasise this point, so perhaps we should not look for too much meaning in it. The demons know who Jesus is: the Son of the Most High God. This is the correct description of him, for it is how the angel Gabriel described him to Mary (1:32), and it is remarkable because the previous story climaxed with the disciples asking 'Who is this?' Their lack of knowledge is highlighted by the fact that Jesus' identity is obvious to the demonic powers.

A 'legion' was a devastating military force of about 6000 Roman soldiers. This clearly suggests that the demons are of great strength; perhaps it is also meant to suggest that the Roman empire, or the military force that maintained it, was evil or demonic. If so, it implies that Jesus has power over that force—which is important given that Jesus will be executed by Roman soldiers amounting to only a tiny proportion of a legion.

Three different groups or individuals respond to Jesus—first, the demons. Despite their immense power, they know that they have to do as Jesus commands (vv. 31–32). Jesus' relationship to them, then, is fundamentally different from his relationship with the others involved—the man, and his neighbours. They are free to choose their response, and the neighbours choose to respond negatively. The message is spread far and wide (the seed is scattered): Jesus has rescued one of them and has driven an evil presence out of their land. Nevertheless, they are afraid and so refuse to respond positively. It is as if they are the 'path' in the parable of the soil. The seed falls on them but is immediately taken away. Jesus accepts their rejection and leaves. The rescued man responds differently. He wants to be one of Jesus' followers. Jesus' reply to him initially seems harsh (v. 39), but in fact the man is given a preaching ministry, just as the apostles and the 72 disciples will soon receive (9:1–6, 10:1–20).

To the natural and spiritual worlds, Jesus simply commands and it is done. Humans, however, are faced with a choice. Why are we treated differently, and do we treat others with the same respect?

4 Two very different women

Luke 8:40–56

This account of one healing as Jesus is on the way to another paints an evocative picture of Jesus' popularity and the demands upon him (which is perhaps why, in verse 56, he attempts to keep people quiet).

The two women have very different places in society. The first woman's prolonged bleeding would have caused her not only physical suffering and embarrassment but also social isolation. It made her 'unclean' in Jewish law and, since 'uncleanness' could be passed on by touch, she would have become an outcast. This is presumably one of the reasons behind her attempt to touch Jesus' cloak anonymously, from behind. In addition, perhaps, she wants to go unnoticed because she feels unworthy of Jesus' attention. However, these negatives are combined with a great faith: she only need touch his cloak anyway (compare the centurion in 7:1–10, another 'polluted' person with great faith).

The woman is healed, but Jesus does not end there. He challenges her low self-esteem. He calls her into the sight of everyone and commends her faith (as he did the centurion's). She does not need to creep around unnoticed. She is as worthy of Jesus' time as is the synagogue ruler. In addition, like the leper in 5:12–14, the woman has been socially isolated, so a full healing of her situation (not just of her illness) will involve her reintegration into society. Thus, it is important that she publicly receives Jesus' declaration that she is 'clean'.

Jairus' daughter, in comparison, has high status as the only child of a leading public and religious figure. Once again, faith is at the heart of the story. The messenger (v. 49) and the mourners (v. 52) do not believe that Jesus can raise the dead, but Jesus urges Jairus to have faith that his daughter can be healed (or 'saved', an alternative meaning of the Greek). Jairus follows the example of the woman who has just been healed from bleeding—perhaps even inspired by her experience—and trusts in Jesus.

Putting the two incidents together, we see that both of the women—one a social outcast, the other the precious daughter of a synagogue ruler—are healed on the basis of faith in Jesus. Do we, in our hearts and in our actions, believe that God treats all equally? Would these two women receive the same welcome and healing in our churches? From a different viewpoint, do we feel like the bleeding woman, needing to hear that we are as worthy of God's attention as the 'beautiful people'—the young, the powerful and the well-connected?

5 Jesus sends out the Twelve

Luke 9:1–9

The Twelve were chosen by Jesus and named envoys ('apostles') in 6:12–16, but now they are sent out to imitate and represent Jesus. They are sent with his power and authority over demons and illnesses, and to preach the kingdom of God—the very activity that Jesus himself was sent for (4:43). Indeed, the fact that Jesus described himself as 'sent' highlights an even closer link between Jesus and the apostles. They are all 'sent'—Jesus by God, the apostles by Jesus—and all have the same work to do and the same authority to do it. It is again noticeable that the proclamation of the kingdom of God goes hand-in-hand with the demonstration of its power.

The restrictions on what the envoys should take with them are harsh: they are to make no preparations at all. This suggests that their task is urgent and also that they should demonstrate in their own circumstances their dependency on God. The instruction to shake off the dust from their feet if they are not welcomed (v. 5) reflects the practice of Jews travelling in Gentile lands, who would shake the dust from their feet when they returned to Israel, to stop the 'unclean' soil from polluting the land of Israel. Thus, Jesus' instruction takes on a grave importance, for it means that the villages who do not welcome his envoys are to be treated as if they were non-Jewish. Those who do not respond to Jesus' messengers are to be treated symbolically as if they are no longer part of God's people.

The mention of Herod in verse 7 can seem out of place. However, it reminds us of two important points. First, John—the one who had prepared for Jesus—has been executed. This casts a shadow over Jesus' seemingly successful mission, which the apostles are now sharing. For all the talk of power and being a messenger of God, there is no guarantee of safety for them. Second, it reminds us of the crucial question 'Who is Jesus?' and that people's response to the apostles' message will be intimately connected to their response to Jesus. Even Herod 'tried to see him' (v. 9) but, when he eventually does meet Jesus (23:6–11), he ends up mocking him.

We are sent out in dependence on God, following the example of Jesus, bringing good news. People will make their choice—a response not so much to us as to Jesus. Some will respond negatively: some seed will fall in unproductive soil. What experience do you have of being Jesus' envoy?

How did you—how should we—cope with the power, the welcome, the rejection and other people's agendas?

6 Feeding in the desert

Luke 9:10–17

The feeding miracle that follows the envoys' return from their mission demonstrates that they are still far weaker than Jesus, and still of limited faith, despite their recent successes. They might have healed people but they do not even pause to think that God can feed the multitude. Jesus, however, very straightforwardly, gets the people to sit down, says a traditional thanksgiving to God for the tiny amount of food that they have, and gives it to the people.

Once again Jesus' power is demonstrated, with a hint towards the Old Testament story of God feeding his people when they were in the desert (the same word as the one used here for a 'deserted place': v. 12; see Exodus 16). This is particularly important because the feeding in the desert happened after the exodus from Egypt, before the Israelites entered the promised land. This would suggest that the 5000 in the crowd have also begun their journey by coming to Jesus but they have not yet reached its goal. God provides food for the journey. It might also suggest, indeed, that Jesus himself has not yet reached his goal. Later in the same chapter Jesus explains what is still to happen, and speaks of the 'exodus' he must accomplish in Jerusalem (9:31).

The feeding story also points back to Jesus' temptation in the desert (4:1–12). There he was tempted to produce food for his own benefit and refused. Now, though, he produces it for the benefit of others. And there is a further reflection on the instructions given to the envoys in the previous passage. If Jesus can provide food for 5000 people in a deserted place, his envoys should certainly have trusted in his provision for them: there really was no need to pack for the journey (9:3).

Some see a reference to the last supper and to the Eucharist in the way Jesus' actions are described: 'blessed... broke... gave' (v. 16; see 22:19). All of us, when journeying in the desert, need the experience of receiving from God (to excess—presumably the message from the leftovers in v. 17), of receiving (in John's words) 'the bread of life' (John 6:48, reflecting on the feeding of the 5000 in 6:1–14). For some, that experience come through the Eucharist; for others, in different ways. Do you take seriously this need to receive sustenance from God? How is that need met in your life?

Guidelines

We are all called by Jesus to journey with him 'on the way'. We are not compelled but invited. All of us are equal in starting out: there are no special favours, special relationships or special knowledge. We are equally worthy of God's attention. We are called to set out on this journey depend-ing solely on God: he will sustain us. Called, equal, worthy, dependent, sustained. How do you relate to each of these ideas, which have emerged from this week's reading? If you say aloud, 'I am called', 'I am equal', 'I am worthy', 'I am dependent', 'I am sustained', what reaction do you have? Do some of these statements stick in your throat or bring emotions to the surface? Why?

28 June–4 July

1 The suffering Messiah

Luke 9:18–27

Peter seems to have grasped who Jesus really is. Going beyond the crowd's identification of him as a prophet, he has recognised that Jesus is God's anointed Messiah (confirmed as the correct understanding at 2:11; 3:21–22; 4:18–19 and 7:18–23). Thus Jesus' reaction (v. 21) seems bizarre. His prophecy about the 'Son of Man' (v. 22) is just as strange, especially when combined with the title 'Messiah'. While the messianic prophecies were open to different interpretations, none suggested that God's anointed was to suffer and die. 'Son of Man' is an ambiguous phrase: it could refer to just 'a human being' or to a 'son of Adam' (implying a fresh start for the human race). In the context of suffering and vindication, though, it is natural to look at Daniel 7, where a figure 'like a son of man' is depicted receiving glory and 'the kingdom' from God, after God's people have endured great suffering. Thus, Jesus would be developing Daniel 7 by including the representative 'son of man' figure in the suffering as well as the vindication.

So, when faced with the title 'Messiah', Jesus points to his own interpretation of Daniel 7, which emphasises that the people of God must undergo suffering before receiving the expected vindication. This explains Jesus' command to silence. The title 'Messiah' is correct but, because it implies no element of suffering, which Jesus sees as an integral part of his mission, it could be misleading.

Jesus does not leave it there. Immediately he unpacks the implication of this revelation for his followers. Earlier the Twelve had been acting as Jesus' representatives, doing the same work as he did (9:1–6). Now comes the negative side of this close association (notice 'for my sake' in verse 24 and 'of me and my words' in verse 26; compare 6:22). The element of surprise that he, as the Son of Man, must suffer is matched by an equal surprise that they, his followers, must suffer too.

The final sentence is striking, raising the obvious question, 'So when did the kingdom come?' By the time the Gospel was written, the majority of those present would have died. Presumably we need to understand 'the kingdom of God' as being seen (at least in part) through Jesus' resurrection—which was the vindication of the Son of Man and the establishment on earth of the new community of God's people. Indeed, we have already seen Jesus and his followers 'proclaiming the kingdom' and manifesting the kingdom through acts of healing and rescue from demons. At least in part, the kingdom can be seen now.

2 The chosen Son

Luke 9:28–36

The transfiguration (which means 'changed appearance') is the key moment of divine revelation in the centre of Luke's Gospel, matching the baptism at the beginning and the events of the crucifixion and resurrection at the end. Here, God acts to reveal the truth about Jesus. First, Jesus is transformed into the appearance of a heavenly being and is seen speaking with the great heroes of old. Then comes the voice from heaven—an even clearer revelation. The words are similar to the divine words at the baptism (3:21–22) but with a crucial difference. There, the voice was only for Jesus to hear ('You are my Son…'); now it is directed to the three disciples ('This is my Son… listen to him)'. Although only the inner core of disciples is present, nevertheless this is the first and only direct testimony by God about Jesus given to others. Indeed, perhaps only his closest disciples—those who have already responded to him—can receive this revelation (8:10, 18). Again Jesus' identity is tied to the need to listen—that is, respond—to him.

Why is the transfiguration reported at this point? Presumably because this revelation confirms the truth of the preceding teaching. The previous passages have been revolutionary. Jesus' response to Peter's proclamation picks up strands from the Old Testament but it is not in keeping with how the Old Testament was understood. Therefore, this divine confirmation of Jesus (and the instruction that the disciples should 'listen to him') validates the surprising teaching that Jesus has just given. What he is saying, and what he is predicting, is the divine will.

There are three other interesting points. First, the presence of Moses and Elijah symbolises the totality of the history of the Jewish people. The story of Jesus is the fulfilment of the Jewish story. Second, they discuss the 'departure' (the word is literally 'exodus') that Jesus will fulfil in Jerusalem. This points to the great saving event in the Old Testament when God rescued his people out of slavery in Egypt and, by so doing, formed a new people, giving them the Law. What Jesus is going to do in Jerusalem will be a fulfilment of the exodus—a new rescue of God's people from slavery, forming a new people, with a new 'law'. Third, Peter does not know what to do, and afterwards they remain silent. The impression is of disciples who are completely out of their depth. Indeed, even after his resurrection, Jesus needs to explain carefully to two of his followers what has really happened (24:13–49). Perhaps we can take comfort in that.

3 The disciples' limitations

Luke 9:37–45

The basic content of this passage is the same as many others: Jesus drives out an evil spirit, demonstrating his authority and bringing rescue to the people involved. The difference in this account, though, is the relationship between Jesus and his disciples. They cannot drive out the demon, despite having been given power to do exactly that (9:1). Jesus seems exasperated with the situation. It is not clear whether it was the disciples who were at fault or whether the problem was that the people had no faith (v. 41) and so the exorcism could not be performed. However, to some extent the disciples must have been at fault, because Jesus was able to cast out the demon even though there was no change in the faith demonstrated by the people or the father. (The father's approach to Jesus may be meant to signify his faith, but presumably he approached the disciples in a similar way.)

The real force behind the exasperation is revealed in the private conversation with the disciples afterwards (vv. 44–45) and the previous passage. Jesus has been planning his 'departure' in Jerusalem. The Son of Man is going to be betrayed. Jesus is not going to be with them for ever. The disciples need to embrace their role as Jesus' envoys and representatives better than this, for soon he will depart and only they will be left. However, the disciples simply do not understand. They do not seem to be up to the particular task required of them (the exorcism) and they do not understand the road of suffering which Jesus is to tread.

The comment that Jesus' meaning 'was concealed from them' (v. 45) seems surprising. Perhaps it is just a turn of phrase indicating that they 'couldn't see it'. It could point to the activity of Satan (as in 8:12, where the devil is said to take away the word from those who have heard), or perhaps it suggests that God hid it from them. If we ask why, the parable of the soil would answer that the disciples are no longer the recipients of the 'secrets of the kingdom' (8:10) because their faith in Jesus and their response to him have waned. The portrayal of the disciples in the previous few passages, and the next one, is hardly positive. Perhaps we too need to take to heart the idea that grasping Jesus' suffering and death is a requirement if we are to work in his name.

4 The disciples' pride

Luke 9:46–56

The disciples' lack of understanding of Jesus and his mission continues in these three short incidents, all of which focus on their pride.

The argument about who is the greatest comes despite the fact that Jesus has twice said that his mission embraces suffering, and that his followers should be willing to give up everything for him (9:24). Jesus' illustration involving the child would have been particularly striking to its original hearers. Today, children are considered especially precious but in the ancient world they were generally seen as the bottom of the heap, to be ignored. Thus Jesus challenges the disciples that they should be focusing on the needs of the unimportant and marginal in the world (compare 4:18–19), for such a person is in fact the greatest. In this way they will be following in the pattern of Jesus, and the one who 'sent' him—God himself.

The unknown exorcist (v. 49) provides a further lesson in pride. Now the disciples are defending their importance as a group against this outsider. They had been given authority to drive out demons (9:1); this was their special role, and they may have been particularly sensitive about it, given their recent failure (9:40). Jesus, however, will not support this kind of exclusivism. They should be pleased that the demon's power is being broken and people are being released, rather than being worried about their own status.

The third lesson comes as Jesus sets off for Jerusalem, embracing the suffering that awaits him. The Samaritans' land was situated between Galilee and Jerusalem, so it was the shortest route to take. The Jewish hatred of Samaritans is expressed in James and John's desire to destroy the village, which would demonstrate their importance as well as confirm their Jewish prejudices. Jesus, however, simply moves on, reflecting the instructions he gave to the disciples at the beginning of the chapter: if a village does not welcome you, move on (while symbolically acting out their rejection of their place among God's people). James and John's desire to treat the Samaritans far more harshly reflects a particular type of nationalistic pride and discrimination, which Jesus rejects.

We can all think of parallels for each of these three demonstrations of pride, in our own lives and the lives of our churches. Perhaps there are people who don't seem to warrant our time and attention; we can be tempted to build up our own importance by claiming that we have exclusive roles (a particular clergy sin); there might be groups in society that we are pleased to criticise or even wish ill of (fundamentalists, liberals, the government, the media, homosexuals, Muslims, old people, the young...). What is our response?

5 The cost of following Jesus

Luke 9:57–62

These three separate incidents, taking place as they walk 'along the road', express further what is required to be a follower of Jesus. The mention of the road reminds us of the suffering Jesus is facing but it could equally be translated as 'the way', which was the name given to the Christian faith in Acts (for example, 9:2; 19:23). The road Jesus travels is 'the way' of his disciples.

In each case, the speakers appear well-intentioned but fail to grasp the absolute commitment required to follow Jesus—particularly a Jesus who is 'on the way' to his death in Jerusalem. The first man claims that he will follow 'wherever you go', and Jesus picks up on this question of place. His reply points to his itinerant ministry, which his followers copy (9:1–6; 10:1–12), a ministry that offers little in the way of security, comfort or even a known place in society. It could also have overtones of his approaching death: the Son of Man is not welcome and will be rejected by this world.

The second man receives the call to follow, just as Levi did (5:27), but he does not simply 'leave everything and follow Jesus' as Levi, Simon, James and John had (5:11, 28). His reason for delay is the most credible, reasonable, pious activity imaginable within that society—and yet it is rejected by Jesus. If burying one's father is not a good reason, nothing is. The need to respond to Jesus and proclaim the kingdom comes above everything.

The third man is similar. He is not even really saying that he has another duty to perform, just that it is appropriate for him to say goodbye, but Jesus has little sympathy. Following Jesus, service in the kingdom, is an all-or-nothing affair. Nothing is more important.

These are perhaps some of the hardest sayings in the Gospel, particularly the middle one. Their extremism (there is no other word for it) cuts across our efforts to 'build a balanced life' and hold different elements—family, friends, work, hobbies, church—in tension. We can at least commit ourselves not to hide from their force or twist their meaning as we seek to face up to their demand and ponder what they might mean for us.

6 The mission expands

'The 72' represent a further expansion of the mission that the Twelve began (9:1–6). The instructions to them are similar, especially about what cannot be taken on the journey. However, the tone is more urgent: they should not even stop to greet people, and the language of harvest points to impending judgment. In the chapter since the Twelve were sent out, much has changed. The general preaching around Galilee is at an end. Jesus is now on the road to Jerusalem, and the 72 are preparing the way. Jesus has already taught that he will find suffering in Jerusalem (9:22, 44) and that his followers face daily trials. Hence it is not surprising that the 72 will face danger as well (v. 3).

The focus of the instructions about lodgings and food is that they can expect to be provided for ('the labourer deserves to be paid') but should accept whatever they are given ('eat what is set before you'). They should not seek to stay with the wealthy or respectable, and they should not be concerned about eating 'unclean food' or with 'unclean people'. Indeed, the only judgment that matters is whether the people accept Jesus' messengers or not.

Verses 8–11 exhibit clearly the double-edged nature of the 'kingdom of God', which connects with the recurring theme in the Gospel that Jesus brings 'the falling and the rising of many' (2:34). In towns that welcome them, the nearness of the kingdom of God is good news, but for those places that do not welcome them it is a threat. Indeed, they are compared unfavourably to the archetypal evil city of Sodom, which was destroyed by God's judgment (Genesis 19). Why? And why condemn the Galilean towns of Korazin, Bethsaida and Capernaum? These places had far more opportunity to respond to Jesus (because of the miracles that were performed in them) than Tyre, Sidon and Sodom. Therefore their lack of response—their refusal to listen, their rejection of Jesus' envoys, of Jesus and of God himself—is all the more wicked.

This is a sobering place to call a halt to our study of Luke. Out attention is drawn once again to the crucial question of how we respond. But now, we are also sharing Jesus' work of announcing the kingdom; we are labourers enduring the same risks as he did.

Guidelines

This week has focused on discipleship—the limitations and pride of the disciples, their role in sharing Jesus' mission, and the cost of being a disciple of the one who, though Messiah and chosen Son, has embarked on a road of suffering.

It is easy to talk glibly about renouncing status, dedication to Jesus and accepting hardship, but these responses are profoundly countercultural. Perhaps there is one that God wants to lay on your heart, not as a command but as a matter to ponder and an area for development as you seek to travel 'on the way' with Jesus. We see in the disciples that it is often as easy to go backwards as to go forwards in these challenging areas. Nevertheless, we are honoured to be chosen as Jesus' messengers, sharing in his announcement of the kingdom.

FURTHER READING

Joel Green, *The Theology of the Gospel of Luke*, CUP, 1995.

Joel Green, *The Gospel of Luke* (New International Commentary on the New Testament), Eerdmans, 1997.

Luke Timothy Johnson, *The Gospel of Luke*, The Liturgical Press, 1991.

Leon Morris, *Luke* (Tyndale New Testament Commentaries), IVP Academic, 2008.

Henry Wansbrough, *Luke* (The People's Bible Commentary), BRF, 1998.

Christopher Tuckett, *Luke* (T&T Clark Study Guides), Continuum, 2004.

Tom Wright, *Luke for Everyone*, SPCK, 2004.

Atonement

I was once involved in conducting a survey of religious views on an outer London housing estate. One of the questions we asked was 'Why did Jesus die?' In most cases the answer came back pat: 'To save us.' (This was back in the 1950s; it might be less predictable today!) But the next question, 'What do you mean by that?', usually produced only a blank look.

The New Testament certainly links our salvation with the death of Jesus, but *how* can the violent death of a village preacher centuries ago affect my standing with God? The problem that faces the interpreter of the New Testament is not lack of explanation but too many explanations, and it isn't easy to place them side by side in a neat, systematic package. The mystery of salvation is too rich and multi-faceted to fit into a single metaphor, and so the New Testament writers drew on a variety of images to try to express its meaning. Temple sacrifice, the law court, personal reconciliation, the freeing of slaves, the conqueror's triumph: these and other areas of human experience have been exploited to try to explain the inexplicable, the unfathomable love of God that overcomes every obstacle to bring sinful human beings back into relationship with their holy Creator.

Over the centuries, sometimes one of these images has appealed most to the church, sometimes another. Christians have sometimes disagreed passionately over which of the images should take priority, but surely the truth of God's reconciling work is too profound to be confined within a single metaphor.

In these two weeks of studies we shall be looking at some of these images as they are developed by different biblical authors. Even these, though, are only a selection. You might well have chosen others. Good! Add your own favourite biblical images. Between us we shall never exhaust the scope of this tantalising but exhilarating puzzle.

Quotations of biblical texts in these studies are from the New Revised Standard Version.

1 'Wounded for our transgressions'

Isaiah 52:13—53:6

It may seem strange to begin a series of studies on the meaning of the death of Jesus by looking at a passage written many centuries before he was born and in which he is not mentioned by name. But from the very beginning, Christians, taking their lead from Jesus himself, have found in this mysterious prophecy a sort of blueprint for the suffering and death of Jesus, who 'bore the sin of many' (53:12). Indeed, many find here a clearer expression of the idea of atonement than any single passage in the New Testament offers.

Was the prophet really writing about Jesus, though? References to God's 'servant' in the book of Isaiah sometimes refer to Israel—the people of God viewed as a corporate whole—but in other places, and especially in these verses, he is apparently an individual who stands over against the people and acts or suffers on their behalf. 'We' (the people) recognise how God has made 'him' (the servant) our representative. Scholars have proposed a reference to a historical individual such as Moses, Hezekiah, Cyrus or the prophet Isaiah himself, but none of them really fits the portrait. It is better seen as a sort of open 'job description', waiting to be embodied. Most Christians would agree that Jesus fits the description better than any other figure we know.

The words are mysterious and there are significant doubts about both the reading of the Hebrew text and its proper translation; hence the striking differences between English versions. But the essential meaning is clear—and startling. Here is a man who does not fit the popular image of a God-given deliverer. Instead of adulation he meets with scorn; instead of triumph he is afflicted, wounded and crushed.

Yet it is in his very suffering and defeat that he has fulfilled his mission. His suffering is vicarious: it was for us that he was ill-treated. He bore our punishment. The people's predicament is described by the imagery of physical illness in verse 4, but the imagery is unpacked in verses 5–6 as that of sin ('transgressions', 'iniquities', 'punishment', 'going astray').

He has taken our place; as a result, we, who deserved to be punished, are 'healed' and 'made whole'. This idea of substitution, of being punished in another's place, will be picked up and developed in some of the New Testament passages we are going to study, but here it is already depicted in the painfully graphic imagery of physical suffering.

2 'A lamb to the slaughter'

Isaiah 53:7–12

The vicarious suffering of God's servant, which was depicted in the first part of the chapter, now takes on the more specific form of martyrdom: the servant is 'cut off from the land of the living'; he 'pours out himself to death'.

The idea that an individual's death could be the means of salvation for others would have been very familiar to the original Jewish readers: the regular ritual of the Jerusalem temple depended on it. That seems to be the background to the servant's role. He is depicted in verse 7 as a sacrificial lamb, and in verse 10 his life is made 'an offering for sin'. Leviticus 1:4 sets out the basic idea of atonement through identification with a sacrificial animal, and Leviticus 4:13–21 designates a single animal as the sin offering for the whole community. What is shockingly different here in Isaiah is that the victim is not a lamb or a bull but a human being.

There is a strange ambivalence in the way his death is described. On the one hand it is the result of violent injustice (v. 8), totally undeserved (v. 9), and yet it is the will of God (v. 10; compare v. 6: 'the Lord has laid on him…'). Even more mysteriously, it is portrayed as an act of the servant's own will ('he poured out himself to death', v. 12); his non-resistance in verse 7 implies as much. Here, then, is much to ponder in relation to the story of how Jesus came to die.

Yet death is not the end. Throughout this passage, and especially in verses 10–12, there runs a note of ultimate vindication and triumph. The suffering and death of the servant have achieved God's saving purpose. Because he is 'righteous', he will in turn 'make many righteous' as he bears their sins and intercedes for them (vv. 11–12). Note the key term 'many', which will be picked up in the New Testament to celebrate the extent of Christ's atonement: one man has died but 'many' are saved (see Mark 10:45; 14:24; Romans 5:15–19).

Isaiah's servant passage is more like an impressionist painting than a pedantically formulated doctrine of atonement—but what an impression! No wonder Christians soon took it as their own. We shall see in the next two studies why they did so.

3 'A ransom for many'

Mark 10:32–45

James and John had a conventional idea of the Messiah's role: to reign in glory. Therefore, they thought, to follow the Messiah was to be on the road to power. However, Jesus has just told them what the road to Jerusalem will mean for him (vv. 33–34). So to follow him is, in fact, to volunteer to share his 'cup' and his 'baptism'—metaphors for the suffering that he must undergo.

In any case, the brothers have the wrong idea about greatness. In the kingdom of God conventional values are turned upside down: greatness is in service, not in being served. Jesus called himself 'the Son of Man', a phrase that evokes the universal rule and authority predicted for 'one like a son of man' in Daniel 7:13 and 14—that 'all peoples, nations, and languages should serve him'. But this 'son of man' has come not to be served but to serve. The model he has set before himself is that of God's servant, and we have seen in Isaiah 53 what that involves—not just serving God but serving God's people, by suffering on their behalf.

So Jesus offers himself as the supreme example of 'service', putting the benefit of 'the many' before his own self-interest, but his words go far beyond any service that James and John could perform. His own act of service is unique and he describes it in words that strongly echo the portrait of God's servant in Isaiah 53:10–12. Like the servant, he will 'give his life', not simply have it taken from him. Those who benefit from his death will be 'many', echoing the words of Isaiah 53:11–12: he 'shall make many righteous… he bore the sin of many'.

To speak of a voluntary death for the benefit of many still leaves a big question mark, though. *How* does his death benefit them? The word 'ransom' introduces another image: the price paid to free a slave. This is the imagery that Paul will develop more fully as 'redemption'. The word itself is not drawn from Isaiah 53 but the idea neatly sums up the effect of the servant's 'sin-offering' (Isaiah 53:10), which results in his people's freedom from guilt and punishment for their sin. Jesus' death will be the sacrifice that sets them free.

4 'My blood... poured out for many'

Matthew 26:26–29

We Christians are so used to our inherited form of worship that we seldom realise what a shocking idea lies at the heart of the Eucharist. 'Eat... my body'; 'drink... my blood': no wonder the early Christians were accused of cannibalism.

To eat bread and drink wine together as a celebration of salvation was a familiar Jewish custom at Passover time, and it was at a Passover meal that Jesus said these extraordinary words. By sharing the flesh of the Passover lamb, whose blood had been smeared on the doorposts, the assembled group identified themselves with the original act of deliverance through which Israel had become the special people of God (Exodus 12:1–14).

Now, though, in place of the lamb was Jesus himself, his death symbolised by the broken bread and the wine poured out. By sharing that bread and wine, his disciples were to identify themselves with the new salvation brought about by Jesus' death.

His body was to be given 'for you' (Luke 22:19) and his blood poured out 'for many', another echo of the language of Isaiah 53:10–12. But this time the purpose of that death is more clearly spelled out: it is 'for the forgiveness of sins' (v. 28), just as the servant in Isaiah's prophecy was to 'bear the sin of many' and so to 'make many righteous'. In the simple words of Mrs Alexander's hymn, 'He died that we might be forgiven; he died to make us good.'

There is another important word in Jesus' saying over the cup. When Israel had been rescued from Egypt, they made their way to Sinai, and there God made a covenant with them to be his special people. That covenant was ratified in a sacrifice and Moses declared, 'See the blood of the covenant that the Lord has made with you' (Exodus 24:8). So now Jesus declares that the wine is his 'blood of the covenant'. Through his death, a new people of God is created under the 'new covenant' that Jeremiah had prophesied (Jeremiah 31:31–34).

5 'He himself bore our sins'

1 Peter 2:21–25

Here is another New Testament Christian meditating on Isaiah's prophecy. Peter is calling on slaves who are Christians to be prepared, if necessary, to accept even unjust suffering. Why should they take such an extraordinary course? Because that is what Jesus has already done, for them.

In words that sound like the personal recollection of someone who saw Jesus on trial and witnessed his amazing silence in the face of maliciously false accusations, Peter emphasises that Jesus' suffering, like that of Isaiah's servant, was undeserved. Yet, like the servant, he accepted it willingly as an act of obedience to the God whose ultimate good purpose he trusted.

Echoes of Isaiah's prophecy ring through the whole passage. It's as if the Peter who once so brusquely rejected Jesus' declaration that the Messiah must die (Matthew 16:21–22) has now had time to think through why it had to happen, and it is in the words of Isaiah that he has found a new and liberating vision of the saving purpose of God.

Verse 24 is one of the New Testament's clearest and most moving assertions that the cross was the place where Jesus 'bore our sins in his body'. It was a sort of exchange: he died so that we might live, and the basis of the exchange is that he took our sins, so that we might be free from them. We shall see similar 'exchange' language in other New Testament passages.

Of course, once such an exchange has taken place we can't just go back to the old life. We live now 'for righteousness'. There is an extraordinary symmetry about the cross: the righteous Jesus is unrighteously killed so that those who have hitherto been unrighteous can live in righteousness (see 1 Peter 3:18 for similar language). This divine logic defies neat systematisation. It calls instead for the grateful wonder with which Peter now meditates on the good shepherd, who has given his life for the sheep.

6 'The righteous for the unrighteous'

Again Peter uses Jesus as an example of undeserved suffering. But verse 18, like 2:24, goes far beyond the fact of undeserved suffering, to explain in a few simple but profound words why he did it. His death was 'for sins'—the theme we have already seen in Isaiah's servant figure, who 'bore the sin of many'. It was 'once for all', not just a stage in an ongoing purpose of salvation: once Jesus has made this one sacrifice, no other is needed. We shall see this theme developed especially in the letter to the Hebrews. There was an exchange of places, 'the righteous for the unrighteous', so that Jesus took on himself what others deserved but he did not. Furthermore, the result of this exchange is 'to bring you to God', to overcome the alienation between sinners and their holy Creator, and thus fulfil God's plan of salvation. It would be hard to improve on this verse as a summary of the doctrine of the atonement in a nutshell.

Peter does not leave it there, however. Verses 18–22 consist of a single complex Greek sentence, which ranges over several loosely related ideas. These verses are so difficult to follow, and have led to so many different interpretations, that unfortunately readers often miss the main triumphant point. As I read the passage, it is a celebration of the fact that Jesus, having been unjustly killed, has been gloriously vindicated through the resurrection and now rules supreme over all the powers of evil. Peter draws on popular Jewish traditions about the fallen angels whose sin was the prelude to the flood (Genesis 6:1–6), and who were believed to be still, even in their imprisonment, the source of evil on earth. But Jesus, through his sacrifice, has triumphed over them, and his people now have nothing to fear. We shall see this theme of triumph through the cross taken up also by Paul in Colossians 2:14–15.

Guidelines

We have seen how Isaiah's 'blueprint' of the servant of God who suffers and dies for the sins of his people influenced both Jesus' own thinking about why he must die and also the mature reflections of one of his leading followers. At the heart of Isaiah's vision is the idea of the exchange of places, of one taking over the responsibilities of another and being prepared to accept the consequences.

Many Christians today are embarrassed or even frankly appalled by this idea of 'substitution' in relation to the consequences of sin. It seems immoral and unjust and suggests an unattractive notion of a God who insists on his 'pound of flesh', whoever it comes from. It may have been all right for the Old Testament Jews, who had been brought up on the idea of animal sacrifice (though even in their scriptures some of the prophets protest that God would rather have moral obedience than sacrifice: see, for example, Hosea 6:6), but surely we have left such 'primitive' ideas behind.

Of course this is only a metaphor and it is dangerous to press a metaphor too hard. In addition, it is only one metaphor among many—but it is undeniably a prominent one in the New Testament.

Here are a few points to consider:

- In this case, the victim is not an unwilling animal but a man who has deliberately accepted the act of self-sacrifice as his God-given mission.
- That man is also the Son of God, so that it is not a matter of God taking it out on a third party but of God absorbing the consequences of sin into himself. The title of Moltmann's book *The Crucified God* gives food for thought.
- On this view, sin is not just brushed aside but faced and dealt with.
- The New Testament presents Jesus' sacrifice as an expression not of God's vengeance but of his love (John 3:16).

As we look at other New Testament images, I hope that they will help to give a wider perspective within which the admittedly difficult idea of vicarious sacrifice can be better understood as one aspect of a multi-faceted truth.

1 'Once for all'

Hebrews 9:11–14

The letter to the Hebrews was apparently written as an emergency measure. The group of Jewish Christians to whom it was addressed seem to have been in serious danger of abandoning their Christian faith altogether and reverting to traditional Judaism. The author (whose identity we don't know) is intent on showing them that at every point where the Old Testament offered something good, Jesus has brought something better. How could they give all that up?

In chapters 7—10 the writer talks about priesthood and sacrifices. Jesus is the one true high priest, who has offered the one supreme sacrifice that now makes all other sacrifices redundant. His sacrifice was 'once for all' (a phrase the author keeps repeating with relish) in contrast with the interminable repetition of animal sacrifices in the temple.

Our author draws especially on the familiar ritual of the Day of Atonement, the one day in the year when the high priest was permitted to enter the Holy of Holies, to make the annual sacrifice that atoned for his own and the people's sins (see Leviticus 16). The old high priests took animal blood into the sanctuary but our author's bold new imagery sees Jesus as carrying his own blood. The same person is both priest and victim. The old animal victims needed to be 'unblemished' but that was a merely physical requirement; this new sacrifice, however, is the morally unblemished Son of God. Whatever efficacy the old sacrifices had in 'purifying' the people is eclipsed by this single sacrifice, which 'purifies our conscience from dead works to worship the living God' (v. 14). The result is not a temporary religious fix but 'eternal redemption'. How could they go back to animal sacrifice after that?

This letter is not easy, and some of the imagery (particularly the insistent focus on 'blood') is frankly unappealing to our ears, but there is no mistaking the triumphant sense of the sufficiency and finality of Christ's saving death, which thrills this creative early Christian thinker.

2 'He sat down at the right hand of God'

Hebrews 10:11–18

These verses are the climax of the long argument in which the author of Hebrews has presented Jesus as the fulfilment of all the patterns and prophecies of the Old Testament, and in particular (in 7:1—10:18) its priesthood and sacrifices.

In verses 11–14 we are reminded of the themes of yesterday's reading. But woven in with the theme of sacrifice and atonement is a note repeatedly sounded by this author as he reflects on Psalm 110, in which the eternal high priest is invited to sit beside the throne of God in the place of supreme authority. Jesus has finished his sacrificial work and now there is, in a sense, nothing to do but sit there and wait (v. 13)—although our author has already reminded us that, as our high priest in heaven, Christ also now represents and intercedes for his people (7:25). Because he is now vindicated and enthroned, his people may follow in full confidence where he has led (10:19–23).

What has been achieved through the 'single offering' of Jesus' sacrificial death is the forgiveness of sins. This is what Jeremiah had envisaged as the heart of the new covenant, and Jesus has already linked the forgiveness of sins with that covenant in Matthew 26:28. In Hebrews 8, the author has quoted Jeremiah's prophecy at length and drawn the conclusion that the establishment of a new covenant means that the old covenant is no longer adequate. Now he rounds off his argument with a reminder of some key phrases in that prophecy. By establishing the new covenant, Jesus has fulfilled God's purpose of salvation and there can be 'no longer any offering for sins' (v. 18). Jesus has done it all. As he exclaimed on the cross before he died, 'It is finished'—or, more idiomatically translated, 'I have done it' (John 19:30).

3 'Justified by his grace'

Romans 3:21–26

We have seen how Isaiah's prophecy of the sacrificial death of God's servant was developed by Jesus in anticipation of his own death and by two of his followers, Peter and the writer of Hebrews, as they tried to explain what his death achieved. Now it is time to turn to the most prolific New Testament theologian: Paul returns to the theme again and again, and we shall look at three sample passages. The first contains (in verses 24–25) probably the most concentrated explanation of salvation through Jesus' death in the whole New Testament.

Paul's question is: how can those who 'have sinned and fall short of the glory of God' (v. 23: that means all of us) nonetheless be restored to 'peace with God' (5:1)? His answer is: not by keeping the law, but 'apart from law' (v. 21), being 'justified by his grace as a gift' (v. 24). Several key words and ideas converge here.

'Justification' (which is the same Greek word as 'righteousness') is a metaphor from the law-court: it means being acquitted, set free from guilt, treated as if 'righteous'. This is a status that cannot be earnt, since no one keeps the law perfectly. Instead, it is an undeserved gift—which is what 'grace' means.

While justification comes free to us, however, it has been 'earnt' by Jesus, who has achieved our 'redemption'. Here is the same idea as the 'ransom' that Jesus spoke of in Mark 10:45, the costly act by which those enslaved (by sin and guilt) are set free.

This redemption was won by Jesus' death (his 'blood'), which provided a 'sacrifice of atonement' (v. 25). Here is the same idea that we saw in Hebrews 9; indeed, the same Greek word is sometimes used for the cover of the ark in the Holy of Holies, the place where the high priest offered the sacrificial blood on the Day of Atonement.

But how can Jesus' death affect our status before God? The whole work of grace is made effective through 'faith'. As we place our trust in Jesus, a relationship is established which enables his actions to apply to us. As Paul will often put it elsewhere, by faith we become 'in Christ', so that he counts for us.

Wow! There's plenty there to think through.

4 'The message of reconciliation'

2 Corinthians 5:11–21

Here in verse 17 is the phrase we noticed at the end of the last study: 'if anyone is *in Christ*'. When that relationship has been established by faith, everything is changed. There is a 'new creation'—a new beginning so radical that it may be compared with what happened in Genesis 1. In this passage Paul reflects on the way such a profound transformation must work itself out in the lives of those who claim that Jesus died for *them*. It makes them 'ambassadors for Christ' (v. 20).

At the heart of this conviction is another key word for our understanding of Jesus' death (repeated five times in verses 18–20): 'reconciliation'. Sin alienates people from the holy God. The whole elaborate sacrificial system of the Old Testament was designed to overcome this alienation, even though, as Hebrews has reminded us, it was not the final solution. Jesus' death, however, has achieved a true 'at-one-ment', a bringing together of those who previously were separated. This is what Paul meant by saying that those who are justified by faith have 'peace with God' (Romans 5:1); this is 'the message of reconciliation'.

Once we have been reconciled with God, it falls to us to 'persuade others' (v. 11) to discover the same reconciliation for themselves. Who else should undertake this task but those who have themselves enjoyed that reconciliation? As Paul reflects on this obligation, he too is drawn to the language of exchange: the sinless one 'became sin' so that the sinful who are 'in him' might 'become righteousness' (v. 21). There is a mysterious symmetry about salvation—except for the point that Paul develops in Romans 5:12–21, that the death of one man has brought salvation to many.

Once the exchange has taken place, those who are 'in Christ' find themselves also sharing in his death (vv. 14–15). They have 'died' to their old lives, but, just as he rose again after death, so now through him they live a new life, not for themselves but for him. Nothing can ever be the same again.

5 'Triumphing in the cross'

Colossians 2:8–15

In these verses we meet again a number of familiar motifs but the passage reaches its climax on a new note, one of defiant triumph over all the powers of evil. We saw a similar idea in 1 Peter 3:18–22. The cross was not a defeat but a victory. It was this paradoxical claim that appealed particularly to some of the early Church Fathers, summed up in the slogan *Christus Victor*.

In verses 12–13 the phrase 'in Christ' again prompts the thought of our identification with the death, burial and resurrection of Jesus. So in verse 13 we are reminded that we were once dead through sin but are now alive with him because our sins have been forgiven. But there is a new note in verse 14–15: what happened to bring this new life about was not a private transaction between Jesus, God and us, but a public confrontation between Jesus and the powers of evil.

The phrase 'the rulers and authorities' refers back to verse 8, where Christ is set over against 'the elemental spirits of the universe', which have their counterpart in human philosophies opposed to God's saving purpose. Paul often speaks of such 'principalities and powers' as the supernatural focus of rebellion against God, the source of evil in what should be a good world. They are what we might call, in less philosophical language, the devil and his angels.

The compressed imagery of verses 14–15 seems to presuppose a court-room scene, where the devil brandishes a charge sheet, according to which we cannot help but be found guilty of disobeying God's law. However, Jesus seizes it and nails it to the cross by taking our place and our punishment. Through his resurrection he then destroys death and so disarms the opposition, exposing the 'authorities' to ridicule. So at the cross the tables are turned and the devil's strategy defeated. The word 'triumph' evokes the vivid picture of the Roman general's victory parade, in which his conquered enemies are humiliated by being dragged through the streets in front of the jeering crowds.

6 'God so loved the world'

John's Gospel has its own remarkable way of speaking about the cross as the place where Jesus was 'glorified' and 'lifted up' (v. 14). Here, that idea suggests a telling parallel from the Old Testament. Moses 'lifted up' a bronze snake on a pole, and all who looked at it were saved from death by snakebite (Numbers 21:6–9). So Jesus, 'lifted up' on the cross, offers eternal life to all who will look at him in faith.

The famous summary of the gospel that follows in verse 16 does not mention the cross, but the fact that it is preceded by verses 14–15 leaves no room for doubt about what it meant for God to 'give' his only Son. God did in reality what Abraham had amazingly been prepared to do until he was mercifully reprieved at the last minute—to sacrifice 'your son, your only son… whom you love' (Genesis 22:2).

John 3:16 does not explain how our salvation was achieved at the cross but it gloriously spells out both the 'what' (eternal life instead of perishing) and the 'why'—the overwhelming love of God. This summary decisively rules out any notion of the atonement as a personal initiative taken by Jesus to buy off an angry God. The initiative is with God himself, rooted in love, not anger. Jesus is 'lifted up' on the cross because his Father has 'given' him as a gift to an undeserving world, which he loved.

The secret of the saving efficacy of Moses' bronze snake was simply a 'look', and the saving efficacy of God's Son lifted up is made available in response to nothing more complicated than 'faith'. To believe is to escape condemnation. Those who, in the end, must face condemnation are not those who have lived conspicuously wicked lives but those who have refused to believe. They have rejected the only solution that God has provided for the problem of sin—the supremely costly gift made available by his love to a world that otherwise must perish.

Guidelines

After such a breathless tour of just some of the different images used in the New Testament to explain what it means that 'Jesus died to save us', it is tempting to try to synthesise them all into a single all-embracing omnibus statement of 'the doctrine of atonement'. But I shall resist that temptation.

Each image, each metaphor, has a life of its own and each contributes something important to our understanding of Jesus' death and our response to it. When you try to fit all the pieces together, though, the edges don't always match. Better to savour each image on its own terms and to recognise the danger of pushing a metaphor outside its own context, or trying to make it answer questions it was not designed to deal with. If you think you have got the doctrine of atonement all tied down in a single formula, however complex, I wonder whether you have really done justice to the multi-faceted nature of the biblical testimony.

We have listened to Isaiah's astonishing prophecy about the servant of God who was to suffer to bring salvation to God's people. We have heard how Jesus drew on Isaiah's words to explain to his disciples why he must die. We have eavesdropped on Peter, Paul, John and the author of Hebrews as they have meditated on different aspects of what it all meant. I hope we have become aware of some common themes that run through these various ways of talking about the basis of our salvation. But none of them, and none of us, can fully do it justice in words printed on a page. There will always be more depths to explore. In the end, the only adequate response is in worship, and in silence—and then in a life lived 'not for ourselves, but for him who died and was raised for us'.

FURTHER READING

David Hillborn, Justin Thacker & Derek Tidball, *The Atonement Debate: Papers from the London Symposium on the Theology of Atonement*, Zondervan, 2007).

Alister E. McGrath, *The Enigma of the Cross* (2nd edition), Hodder & Stoughton, 1996.

Scott McKnight, *A Community Called Atonement*, Abingdon Press, 2007.

I. Howard Marshall, *Aspects of the Atonement: Cross and Resurrection in the Reconciling of God and Humanity*, Paternoster Press, 2007.

Tom Smail, *Once and for All: A Confession of the Cross*, DLT, 1998.

John R.W. Stott, *The Cross of Christ* (3rd edition), IVP, 2006.

Psalms 1—13 (12)

The Psalter is Israel's prayer book but also the prayer book of the Church. Ancient tradition attributes authorship of the psalms to King David, but this is quite certainly wrong, for some of the psalms are ancient Canaanite hymns to their god Baal, later slightly modified for Israelite worship, and some of them mention the exile in Babylon. The tradition merely reflects the reverence for David as founder of the temple liturgy. We do not know how the psalms were collected, how they were selected or how they were preserved—presumably in the temple. Like many collections of religious poetry, they express many moods, reflect on many situations and fit many different occasions. They cover, then, the whole sweep of Israel's history and spirituality. More than this, the psalms were the prayers of Mary and Jesus: Mary's Magnificat is shot through with reminiscences of the psalms, and Jesus is shown in three of the Gospels as dying with a psalm-prayer on his lips.

As early as Peter's speech at Pentecost, the psalms began to be used (often stretching their original sense a little) to explain and comment on the resurrection and exaltation of Jesus. This fuller, Christian sense of the psalms is part of the treasury and prayer of the Church.

A note on numbering: These notes are based on the Revised Grail Psalter, which, in accordance with the Roman Catholic tradition, uses the numbering of the Greek version of the Psalms, rather than the Hebrew. In the Greek text, the Hebrew Psalms 9 and 10 are shown as a single psalm—Psalm 9. Thus the Greek version stays one number behind until Psalm 148. Because many Protestant versions adopt the Hebrew numbering (following Luther's preference), however, both numbers have been given in psalm references between 10 and 147. You will find the Hebrew number given first, with the Greek in brackets afterwards.

Quotations from the Psalms are taken from the Revised Grail Psalter; other biblical references are from the New Jerusalem Bible.

1 'Blessed indeed is the man'

This psalm is carefully placed at the beginning of the Psalter. It is a Wisdom psalm. A great deal of the Wisdom literature at the end of the Old Testament period gives rules and hints about how to get on in life. Much of the advice is in the form of wise proverbs, not always particularly religious: 'Bread is sweet when it is won by fraud, but later the mouth is full of grit' (Proverbs 20:17). However, through it all runs the thread that all wisdom comes from the Lord.

Sorting the psalms into categories sometimes contributes to easier understanding. Several of the psalms fall into this category of celebrating the blessing on those who set themselves to fulfil God's Law. Such psalms often begin, 'Blessed are those who…' (for example, Psalms 32 [31] and 41 [40]). Two of the special Wisdom psalms are our present psalm and the lengthy Psalm 119 (118). It has been suggested that they were placed at the beginning and end of a primitive collection of psalms as a sort of inclusive literary bracket, thus stressing the importance of observing the Law for all prayer and service.

These psalms of the Law are joyful psalms, for obedience to the Law is a joyful response in love to a gift in love. The Law is no burden but a pleasure and privilege. It is God's set of instructions on how to remain close to God, given to his own special people. It is both a gift in friendship and a revelation of God's own nature. Obedience to the Law is a matter of imitation of God: 'Be holy as I am holy' is the theme song of the Law in Leviticus. Obedience is not a way of earning salvation but is a loving response to God's gift in friendship, and so full of joy.

This little psalm conceals its artistry. First comes the blessing on those who stand apart from sinners and delight in the Law. Then there is an image for this blessing—the tree planted beside flowing waters. In a dry land, water is the secret of life and not every tree flourishes. I think especially of a particular tree, growing luxuriously beside the sparkling stream that runs from the Ain Qilt down to Jericho. It always has a flock of sheep and goats enjoying its shade.

Then, in verse 4, the opposite of blessing is described, in the opposite order: first comes the image, chaff blown away by the wind, then the description of the wicked. Finally, the last verse sums up the message with a neat contrast.

2 'Why do the nations conspire?'

Psalm 2

Originally this psalm was a coronation-song. The death of a king and the succession of a new monarch was frequently the signal for rebellion by subject peoples, whom the Lord here 'laughs to scorn' (as Handel's *Messiah* puts it), for the Lord himself has decreed and anointed the new king. The ritual of kingship in Jerusalem took over a great deal of the Egyptian coronation ritual. On the great Egyptian wall-carvings the king is shown being anointed and crowned by the deities of Upper and Lower Egypt. In the Egyptian ritual of coronation, the king also became son of the gods.

In Israel, of course, this divine sonship had a different root—God's promise to David, through Nathan, of a dynasty which would never end (2 Samuel 7:4–17). David offered to build a house for the Lord, but the Lord replied with a promise to build David a house, with his own son as his successor: 'I shall be a father to him,' he promised, 'and he a son to me' (v. 14). Though the Lord might punish the king, he would never withdraw his love. This promise is the basis of Israel's security and of the enduring hope for a Messiah who would rule the nations. The same promise is celebrated in another coronation-psalm, Psalm 110 (109), and is frequently alluded to elsewhere in the Bible. During the exile, Psalm 89 (88) meditates on the failure of the kingship and reproaches God for reneging on his promise.

The Christian tradition, beginning with the letter to the Hebrews (1:5), sees this promise as fulfilled in Christ. Jesus himself was hesitant about the title 'son of God', never openly accepting it. When Peter at last recognises Jesus as 'the Christ', Jesus reacts not with congratulations but with a warning that he is to triumph only after suffering (Mark 8:29–31). When the high priest challenges Jesus, 'Are you the Christ?' Jesus replies by diverting attention to his favourite title, 'the son of man' (Mark 14:61–62). This is probably because of the political associations of the concept of Messiah at the time, as an anointed king who would expel the Romans. For Jesus, it is not his own kingship but the kingship of God that fills his horizon.

Nevertheless, as early as Paul, 'Christ' (the Greek equivalent of the Hebrew 'Messiah') has become a standard name for Jesus. At Antioch, the great Jewish colony where Paul set up his first base for the proclamation of the gospel, the followers of Jesus first gained the name (possibly a slightly derisory nickname) 'Christians'—those who acclaimed Jesus as Messiah. They saw in Jesus the fulfilment of the anointed king promised in this psalm.

3 'How many are my foes, O LORD!'

Psalm 3

This is the first of the 'Psalms of David', a series that runs to Psalm 41 (40). The title added later at the head of each of these psalms attributes them to David and usually situates them at some particular moment in David's life. These indications are not to be taken too seriously. The situating of this psalm—'When he was fleeing from his son Absalom' (that is, when Absalom had rebelled against his father and made a bloodless entry into Jerusalem)—is particularly forced.

This is also the first of the psalms of confidence in distress, a frequent motif in prayer. It raises again the unanswerable question of how the psalms were preserved and used. Were psalm sheets kept in the temple and handed out on request to worshippers who asked for a particular type of prayer? That seems too modern an idea. In any case, we cannot tell. Sometimes the psalms seem to concentrate too much on the negative side of life. However, we are all drawn more quickly to prayer by threats to our comfort and prosperity! The calm confidence of the psalmist, who is content to brave the threats of the surrounding legions of enemies and go quietly to sleep, is a model for Christian trust in the Lord.

'I shall awake, for the Lord sustains me' (v. 5) is, by extension, understood in the Christian tradition as an allusion to Christ's resurrection. The verb used for 'awake' in the Greek is often used also of the resurrection.

The doctrine of the resurrection of the dead becomes clear only in Daniel 12:2–3, written a couple of centuries before Christ, but the Greek Bible (particularly in the psalms) shows many signs of a tradition developing towards that belief. The translations chosen for the Greek Bible (the original Bible of the Christian Church) are a valuable indication of the developments of thinking within Judaism, and many regard the so-called Septuagint as an inspired translation. There is a longing for the continuance of a relationship with God instead of the unsatisfactory, powerless half-life in Sheol, where no one can praise God. With this longing goes a groping towards the belief in resurrection, in the form of a conviction that God will not abandon his chosen ones. As Jesus says in reply to the Sadducees, 'He is God, not of the dead, but of the living' (Matthew 22:32).

4 'When I call, answer me, O God of my righteousness'

Psalm 4

This psalm is built on a contrast between trust in the Lord to provide what is needed and a certain materialistic preoccupation with acquiring the good things of this world. The psalmist is confident that the Lord hears prayers and grants what is needed. The opening mention of 'distress' is hardly sufficient to suggest upset or discomfort; it simply makes us aware that the Lord's protection is needed and is forthcoming.

The psalmist is sure that the Lord works wonders for his faithful ones; the Lord 'listens when I call to him' (v. 3). What exactly is this sureness of answer to prayer, and can we count on it so securely? How does God manage it if I want a fine day for my cricket match and the neighbouring farmer wants rain for his crops? A mature Christian may still desperately want something and pray for it fervently, but all the while his or her prayer includes an implied conditional clause: 'if it is your will and plan'. The mature Christian is still a child of God, turning to the Father in confidence but also in realisation that no human being can fully understand God's purposes. The sufferer who goes in fervent and desperate prayer to a healing shrine such as Lourdes may not be granted the cure they sought but does win at least the strength to endure, and perhaps to understand, the suffering. In the last analysis there will always be cases where the book of

Job provides the only solution: we cannot understand God's reasons but are enabled to bow before the vision of his wisdom and greatness.

By contrast, those who do not have this confidence are heavy of heart and chase after illusions, all the while complaining that no one offers them happiness. There is a touch of humour in the contrast between their frenetic and grumbling pursuit of happiness and the psalmist's contented and simple relaxation in the Lord. There is also a touch of irony in the fact that these seekers after happiness in material wealth also invoke the Lord in their search, expecting it to be given them on a plate and asking to bask in the light of his face. Yet their plentiful harvest of corn and new wine does not bring them the contentment that the psalmist wins by trust in God.

The mention of keeping silence 'on your beds' (v. 4), and of falling asleep and resting secure (v. 8), suggests that the time of praying is evening, after a day spent in awareness of divine protection.

5 'To my words give ear, O LORD'

Psalm 5

This is a simple morning prayer, rejoicing in the protection of the Lord at daybreak, contrasting the favour of the Lord toward his faithful with the Lord's detestation of evildoers, liars and the violent. The psalmist has a reassuring confidence in God's response to prayer and the closeness of God to those who come to pray to him. There is, however, a note that falls badly on the Christian ear—the appeal to God for judgment on the evildoers' guilt. It is not even an appeal for personal vengeance on unfair treatment, but seems quite unprovoked—apart from a passing reference to 'those who lie in wait for me' (v. 8).

It is possible to consider this jarring note as an expression of the desire for the annihilation of evil itself, a pious prayer that justice may triumph. More honest, however, is the admission that this desire for vengeance does exist in Old Testament morality. 'An eye for an eye, and a tooth for a tooth' (Deuteronomy 19:21b) was already an advance on a morality where there were no limits to revenge exacted, where someone could be killed for the sake of an eye or a tooth. The Psalter leaves no doubt that Israel found it reasonable actually to pray for vengeance, as the so-called 'cursing psalms' show. The haunting Psalm 137 (136) ends with a blessing on those who dash Babylonian babies against a rock, and Psalm 109 (108) is (from the literary point of view) a deliciously and artistically comprehensive curse on the psalmist's enemies.

It was Jesus who outlawed all forms of revenge, with his command to 'love your enemies and pray for those who persecute you' (Matthew 5:44). The desire for vengeance is a very deep-seated human instinct. We must, furthermore, grant that revelation is a slow process and, at the same time, admit that we have no reason to believe that we have yet have reached the full implications of Christ's teaching. We cannot take on board too much at one time. Despite the implications of Pauline teaching, for many centuries Christendom continued to tolerate slavery and enjoy its benefits. For many centuries war and its accompanying slaughter were considered an acceptable last resort for solving disagreements under certain circumstances (the criteria of 'just war' theory). Even in the last decade, Christian leaders have instigated a war whose 'justness' has been questioned. The suitability of the death penalty as the ultimate punishment is also still debated among Christians and non-Christians alike.

6 'O LORD, do not reprove me in your anger'

Psalm 6

This is the first of the psalms of real distress, expressed with extreme drama or perhaps even exaggeration. Then suddenly it issues in a sharp turnaround, to confidence that the Lord has heard the prayer and already solved the problem.

These two phases are characterised respectively by the Lord's anger and his faithful love. The psalmist does not deny that punishment is due, but begs to be spared and appeals to God's faithful love, finally thanking God for deliverance from the threatening disasters. How can these two fit together?

The anger of the Lord is, of course, an anthropomorphism. Another anthropomorphic expression for it is the Lord's 'jealousy'. Frequent enough is the declaration that God is a jealous God. Divine jealousy is not like human jealousy. Human jealousy is hankering after qualities or possessions that one sees in others. Divine jealousy is a refusal to tolerate the attribution to other values of the honour or obedience due to God, particularly if such honour is attributed to other deities—personifications of other systems of value. It is a refusal, therefore, to tolerate upset in the due order of the world, of which God is the ultimate guarantor. God's 'anger' is the attribution to God of the human emotion that so often precedes and occasions punishment.

The paradox is at its sharpest in the revelation to Moses at Sinai of the meaning of God's special, personal name. After the Israelites have broken the covenant and Moses has smashed the tablets of the Law, God passes before Moses crying out, 'The Lord, the Lord, God of tenderness and compassion, slow to anger, rich in faithful love and constancy... yet letting nothing go unchecked, and punishing...' (Exodus 34:6–7). This is the definition of God that echoes down scripture, alluded to again and again throughout the Old Testament. The paradox consists in the juxtaposition of compassion and punishment. How can God punish and yet be compassionate? Is God's forgiving punishment less severe than it should be? Hardly, if the punishment is intended to be therapeutic. Perhaps it is like a loving father who punishes to bring the recalcitrant child back to the true path, but can lighten the punishment without reducing its effect by simultaneously showing the reality of his love, in some way sharing the child's pain.

Guidelines

In this first small group of psalms we have already seen the richness and diversity of the relationships expressed in this collection of Israel's prayers. The first psalm introduces the collection. The second presents the theme of messianism, leading to the central position of Christ, which for Christians is at the heart of all prayer. The other four show some of the different aspects of our relationships to God, the varied moods in which we pray, the problems we bring, and the complications of life that draw us to prayer.

A recurring theme can perhaps be identified, however—confidence in God. How confident are we in God's closeness, his compassion, his ability to answer prayer and bring resurrection? Are we confident enough in his provision to resist the urge for revenge and rest content with the gifts he has given us? If so, we too can flourish like the 'tree planted near streams' (Psalm 1:3).

1 'O LORD, my God, I take refuge in you'

Psalm 7

This psalm may be seen as falling into three distinct but related parts. Verses 1–5 form an appeal to the Lord for protection, suggesting that the psalmist is being pursued by someone whom he attacked, though the attack does not seem to have been unprovoked. Verses 6–12a appeal to God specifically as a just judge, who can be relied on to reward integrity and punish the opposite. Verses 12b–16 somewhat return to the first part, stressing the justice of God in foiling the unprovoked attack of an enemy. Finally the psalmist sums up the prayer in a verse of praise for God's saving justice.

God's justice is understood throughout the Bible in two senses. Firstly, God is a just judge in the ordinary sense of the word, assessing merits and faults and assigning their just rewards; this is the sense found in the second part of the psalm. Secondly, but perhaps more importantly, God's justice is a saving justice. It is often put in parallel with 'salvation' or 'deliverance', as in Isaiah 46:13, 'I am bringing my *justice* nearer… my *salvation* will not delay'.

Human justice consists in conformity with the law (observing speed limits) or moral demands (repaying debts), but God's justice is observance of his own promises. For the Israelite, and subsequently for the Christian, God's saving justice does not condemn us for our failures but quite the reverse: it is our only hope. God can be relied upon to fulfil his promises, especially the promises made to Abraham and the promises involved in the series of subsequent covenants to David and Jeremiah, and finally the new covenant in Christ's blood. All we can do is put our trust in this saving justice of God.

Paul meditates on this saving justice in the letter to the Romans: 'Abraham put his faith in God and this was reckoned to him as saving justice' (4:3). Human 'justice' cannot be earnt by good deeds but is simply a matter of hanging on by our fingertips to God's saving justice—that is, trusting in his promises to save. We are justified—that is, put in a state of salvation—only by being clothed with God's own saving justice. In the last analysis, God's promises are fulfilled by Jesus' obedience on the cross, which 'fulfils all justice'. We profess our faith in and our dependence on that obedience by being baptised into Christ's death, and so bathed with his saving justice.

2 'O Lord, our Lord, how majestic is your name!'

Psalm 8

This joyful psalm is a celebration of the creation, bracketed at beginning and end by praise of God's majestic power. The first creation story in Genesis has the appearance of narrating what happened long, long ago. In fact, it is a theological statement in story form of the present, permanent relationship of the universe as we know it to the divine power that even now holds it in being. Psalm 8 is not an account but a celebration of that relationship. By its very being, the creation praises God: even the mouths of infants who cannot yet articulate words praise God in a way quite sufficient to confound his enemies.

Three little points may add to our appreciation of this psalm. First, the order differs from the account in Genesis. Human beings remain the crown of creation, made in God's image, but the order is different. In Genesis, the climax comes at the end of the creation story; here, human beings come immediately after the creation of the heavens and are followed, not preceded, by the animal creation.

Second, what are we to think of the phrase 'little less than the gods' (v. 5)? Is this an assertion that other gods exist? No; rather, it is using the language of the surrounding peoples and indeed the Canaanites, who honoured or worshipped a variety of divinities. Baal, the chief god of Canaan, was a storm-god, represented as hurling a bolt of forked lightning. Often, Hebrew literary forms lean towards such language, sometimes comparing these gods to the Lord, sometimes downgrading them to the status of angels. The letters to the Colossians and Ephesians take stock of the situation explicitly: in Christ everything has its being. 'Everything visible and everything invisible, thrones, ruling forces, sovereignties, powers—all things were created through him and in him' (Colossians 1:16).

Third, the psalm is playfully anthropomorphic: the heavens were shaped by the fingers of God (v. 3). The beginning and end are more theological: the praise is given to the name of the Lord. The name of the Lord bespeaks the divine power. When God reveals the meaning of his name to Moses (Exodus 34:5–7), he reveals the nature of his saving power. In Isaiah we read, 'I am the Lord; that is my name! I shall not yield my glory to another' (42:8). In the same way, in Acts, Christians are baptised 'into the name of the Lord Jesus' (see 10:48; 19:5), and are those over whom the name of Jesus has been called. That is, Christians are those who put themselves under the power of Jesus.

3 'I will praise you, Lord, with all my heart'

Psalms 9—10 (9)

Here begins the dislocation of numbering, for Psalm 9 in the Greek version is divided into Psalms 9 and 10 by the Hebrew. The Greek version, the original Bible of the Christian Church, represents the state of the Hebrew in the second century before Christ, so the division in the present Hebrew text must have been made after that. Further indication that the whole poem was originally one comes from the lettering. The psalm is an alphabetical psalm—that is, each quatrain begins with a different letter of the Hebrew alphabet, working through to the end. In other psalms the same neat device is used—for example, in Psalm 111 (110) there is a new letter for each line; in Psalm 119 (118) stanzas of eight lines begin with the same letter.

The psalm is redolent with the spirituality of the Lord's care for the orphan, the oppressed, the needy and the poor. Although God's care for the poor is a theme that runs throughout Israel's literature, pre-exilic spirituality is rather more robust: material success is a blessing from the Lord. From the exile onwards, Israel was more conscious of its own failures and of its continuously oppressed state. The exiles had lost their confidence and concentrated on their guilt, continually expressing their repentance. This was reinforced by circumstances. First there was the state of servitude in the Babylonian exile. Then, after the return to Judea, came harassment from those who had stayed behind or had been transported there, and oppression by one foreign power after another—Greeks, Egyptians, Syrians, Romans. So in their enforced humility the Israelites saw that this itself was a blessing, that the blessing of the Lord is upon those who trust not in themselves but in God's own saving power. The poor of the Lord are under the shelter of his wings and under the special blessing of his hand.

This spirituality receives its full expression in the prophets of this period, especially Zephaniah. The poor of the Lord are those who accept this state of dependence and put all their trust in God's power and willingness to save: 'Seek the Lord, all you humble of the earth' (Zephaniah 2:3). God declares, 'I shall leave surviving a humble and lowly people, and those who are left in Israel will take refuge in the name of the Lord' (3:12–13). This line of thought runs straight through to the Beatitudes in Luke ('Blessed are you who are poor', 6:20) and to Mary's canticle of the Magnificat.

4 'In the LORD I have taken refuge'

Psalm 11 (10)

This psalm of confidence is based on the presence of the Lord among his people. Is this presence 'in heaven' or 'in his holy temple' (v. 4)? The lines and the thoughts are in parallel, a frequent phenomenon in Hebrew poetry—or, rather, the one widespread structural element of Hebrew poetry. While English poetry often achieves its balance by a rhyming syllable at the end of the line, Hebrew poetry gains its balance by parallelism. Two lines make roughly the same statement: for example, 'O God, come to my assistance // O Lord, make haste to help me.' Sometimes one of the two statements is phrased negatively: 'Lord, deliver me from my enemies // do not let them triumph over me.' This gives a satisfying rhythm. In the case of this psalm, whether the Lord is in his temple or in the heavens, the assertion is that the Lord is in control.

The psalm expresses in several different ways the protective presence of God. This is a fundamental theme in the Bible. His eyes watch over the world (v. 4) and, conversely, the upright will ever see his face (v. 7). On Sinai Israel experienced the presence of God among them, choosing them to be his own people. He remained present among them, and Moses went to consult him in the ark of the covenant, housed in the middle of the camp, in the tent of meeting. It was an awesome encounter. The splendour of the Lord was such that Moses subsequently had to keep his face veiled (Exodus 34:33): 'the Israelites could not look Moses steadily in the face' (2 Corinthians 3:7). When David had captured Jerusalem and made it his capital, he made it also God's capital by bringing the ark, the presence of God, into Jerusalem. It was a protecting presence but a presence not to be trifled with, as the fate of Uzzah showed (2 Samuel 6:7).

In the Gospels it is perhaps Matthew who most stresses this presence, which is now the divine presence of Jesus in his Church. Jesus' name, 'Emmanuel', means 'God with us' (Matthew 1:23), and 'Where two or three meet in my name, I am there among them' (18:20). Again in Matthew, corresponding to the initial bracket of 'Emmanuel' is the final bracket, as Jesus, the risen Lord and glorious Son of Man, sends out his apostles, promising, 'I am with you always, to the end of time' (28:20).

5 'Save me, O LORD'

Psalm 12 (11)

The sadness that the psalmist feels here stems from being enmeshed in a web of lies. To be misrepresented or misunderstood is an ultimate frustration, and here it seems that the false representation is being passed round deliberately, maliciously and rapidly. A right to truth and a good reputation is one of the basic human rights, without which no security is possible. It is one of the major social values, put forward by the Ten Commandments themselves, and the psalmist longs for it, contrasting the web of lies with the pure silver of God's truth, truthfulness and trustworthiness—to which he applies the lovely image of sparkling silver 'seven times refined' (v. 6).

Another 'gold standard' (or perhaps we should say 'silver standard') enters into the calculations here, namely salvation. The first word of the psalm is 'Save!' and verse 5 repeats this confidence in the Lord's 'salvation'. Here the salvation envisaged is obviously rescue from deceit and misrepresentation, but in Christian prayer the concept is used widely and often thoughtlessly. What does God save us from? From hell, from evil, from slavery to sin, from enemies, from poverty and oppression, from ourselves? Is the basic worry about threatening disaster an unnecessary pessimism for Christians? The image of God as Saviour stems originally from God's rescue of Moses and his people from slavery in Egypt—the great salvation of the exodus. A repetition of this rescue was Israel's expectation in the dark days of the Babylonian exile.

Primarily the Saviour is God, and the title is transferred to Jesus only rarely in the New Testament. In the Gospels it is used almost exclusively by Luke. He uses the concept of Jesus (the name means 'Saviour') in contrast to the saviour-gods of the Roman world. In that uncertain world of unpredictable disaster, it was common to be initiated into cults of mysterious magical deities that promised stability and safety. Luke presents Jesus as the only true Saviour. Jesus travels through Galilee rescuing people from all the fears of sickness, death, alienation, addiction, unknown and threatening powers and taboos, emptying the worm-can of fear. Whatever we fear, Jesus is ultimately the guarantor of liberation and salvation.

6 'O LORD, will you forget me for ever?

Psalm 13 (12)

In this neat little psalm the psalmist is intensely personally preoccupied. In almost every line, 'I', 'me' or 'my' occurs. It is an energetic, vigorous poem, and its thought advances by hammering repetition. First comes a fourfold 'How long…?' (vv. 1–2). Then there are three insistent imperatives—'look', 'answer', 'give light' (v. 3)—followed by three dangers to be avoided: 'or I shall fall… or my foe will boast… my enemy have the joy of seeing me stumble' (vv. 3b–4). Only after this fusillade of hammer-blows does the psalmist relax in the final verse by putting all trust in the salvation and in the *hesed* of God.

This *hesed* is a key concept for Israel. It is normally translated 'faithful love' or 'merciful love', but it is a concept that grips and warms the heart. In origin it is the love that binds together a close and devoted family, in which every member can count on the inalienable support of each one. The concept is enshrined in Israel's family law, protecting against ultimate disaster. If a brother marries and dies without children, his brother must marry the widow and raise up a child in the dead brother's name. If a brother falls on such hard times that he is forced to sell his share of the ancestral land, the nearest brother must buy it back for him. Each member of the family can rely on the fact that they may not get on very well with one another but, in the last analysis, they won't let each other down. Hesed is the love of the mother who will never turn her child away, whatever hurt the child does to her. So unalterable is God's love, the love of the father for the prodigal son, and that is why we can 'trust in your faithful love'.

Hosea is the prophet of such love, and it is from Hosea 6:6 that Jesus takes his text, 'What I want is love, not sacrifice.' In Matthew this principle is repeated three times (9:13; 12:7), forming the touchstone for the application of the Law. The Father's unalterable love does not spawn a formal, ritual response, but evokes a heartfelt, reciprocal love of God and of the neighbour as oneself.

Guidelines

In these prayers of Israel, handed down generation after generation, we see many aspects of God's love, many treasured ways in which Israel conceived and honoured her saving God. Like our own, Israel's relationship with God could be tempestuous—by turns rebellious and trusting, devoted and disobedient. These concepts also formed the background of Jesus' prayer. Many of them he merely made his own; some he developed and enriched, giving us further insights for our own approach to God. It is fitting, therefore, that they should be also the backbone of Christian prayer. By making these prayers our own, we enter more deeply into Jesus' own experience of his Father.

Biblical ethics and Christian discipleship

How shall we therefore live? In a post-Christian society, this question is crucially important and difficult. It is important for Christians if they are to live lives that provoke questions from others and attract them to Christ. It is important for those who are not Christians but seeking for wisdom and direction as to how to live well.

Because we have a gospel of grace, we often downplay the significance of ethics and Christian discipleship. We therefore risk offering what the great German theologian Dietrich Bonhoeffer called 'cheap grace' rather than 'costly grace'. We need to remember that Paul frames Romans, the great letter of justification by faith not works, with his quest for 'the obedience of faith' (1:5; 16:26) and is clear that we are redeemed so that 'we may bear fruit for God' (7:4).

This week's readings seek to provide a biblical framework for thinking theologically about ethics and discipleship. We begin in the Old Testament with the Decalogue. This gives concrete commandments but roots them in the character of the covenant God, who speaks to his people and is concerned with our heart as well as our actions. Jesus highlights that focus on the heart in the Sermon on the Mount, in which he radicalises the Law that he came to fulfil. With Christ, we are no longer simply following rules and laws but following a person. Our third passage therefore focuses on Jesus' call to discipleship, which means that we are no longer to follow our own desires or the way of the world. The positive pattern of this call is summed up in Jesus' teaching about the greatest commandment—love of God and love of neighbour.

As Christian communities put that love into practice today, we can learn from Paul's shaping of the moral vision of the first churches in Ephesus and Rome. He sketches the virtues of character and patterns of community that Christians should display, and guides us in facing new challenges and questions. Ephesians 4 provides a key test for any claim to be following Jesus—'Is this pattern of life worthy of our calling?'—while Romans 12 gives us three disciplines that enable us to discern God's will.

Quotations are taken from the New International Version of the Bible.

1 The Ten Commandments

Exodus 20:1–21

I wonder how well you score? Not on keeping the commandments but knowing them! In June 2009, a survey commissioned to promote a new computer game reported that more than a quarter of British 11- to 16-year-olds cannot recall any of the Ten Commandments. The Decalogue, should, however, play a central part in Christian ethics—even though we must not reduce ethics to laws and commandments.

The introduction to the commandments is as important as the commandments themselves. Verse 1 highlights their seriousness—God himself has spoken them directly—but verse 2 is crucial. These are not the words of some unknown God; nor are they simply a universal moral code. The God who speaks is clearly identified as the covenantal God: 'I am the Lord your God.' We can easily forget, given the experience of Christendom and the historic place of the Decalogue in Western society, that the commandments are set in the context of divine election. We should not be surprised if living by them makes us different.

The God who speaks is the redeeming God who liberates slaves. This gives a central framework for Christian ethics: how we are to live is rooted in and shaped by the prior liberating work of God. Only when we know that we have been freed from slavery can we begin to learn the shape of the obedience for which we have been freed.

The commandments themselves begin with the need to relate rightly to this God: ethics cannot be separated from worship and spirituality. Humans are inherently worshipping and serving creatures, and our first challenge is to worship and serve the true God, not idols (vv. 3–6). We then need to examine how we speak of God (v. 7) and ensure that our working lives mirror or image God (see Genesis 1:28) in a balance that values sabbath rest for all in society (vv. 8–11). The next five commandments identify aspects of life where we need to show respect and honour—in relation to parents, human life, sex and marriage, others' property and the truth (vv. 12–16). The final commandment is one that some Jewish and Christian commentators see as climactic. It addresses the root failing that leads us to violate the preceding commandments—desire for that which is not properly ours (compare Colossians 3:5). Here we see that God's concern and our ethical challenge are not ultimately a matter of rules but a matter of the heart.

2 Being salt and light: Jesus' interpretation of Law

Matthew 5:13–30

If the Decalogue is the charter of ethics for the people of God in the Old Testament, the Sermon on the Mount has that standing for the new covenant people of God in Christ. It is the first of Matthew's five discourses (echoing the five books of Moses: the other four are chs. 10, 13, 18 and 24—25) and it, like the Law, was given on a mountain.

Following Jesus' vision of the fulfilled life of happiness in the Beatitudes (5:1–12), the opening words of today's reading reaffirm the distinctive lifestyle of God's people: we are called to be salt and light (vv. 13–14). The goal of this differentiation is not to be separatist or sectarian withdrawal from the world. The goal is missional engagement in the world: 'that they may see your good deeds and glorify your Father in heaven' (v. 16).

How does this relate to the Decalogue? Jesus clearly rejects the abolitionist view that grace and the kingdom of heaven simply dispense with law. Instead he calls his disciples to see him as bringing the Law to its goal and fulfilment. Far from disregarding the pattern of righteousness found in Israel's scriptures, Jesus' followers are to surpass its standards (vv. 17–20).

This teaching is illustrated with reference to the two commandments relating to human life and marriage and sex. Jesus interprets them in the light of yesterday's conclusion that the heart's desire is crucial to faithfulness and holiness. Twice using the contrast 'You have heard that it was said… But I tell you…' (vv. 21–22, 27–28), he radicalises and internalises the prohibitions against murder and adultery. The heart of the human ethical problem is identified as the ethical problem of the human heart.

God's goal is not simply to get us to refrain from killing or sleeping around with each other. These violations of God's law derive from vices and sicknesses that go deeper than mere actions. Jesus points to anger and lust, two of the 'seven deadly sins' in Christian tradition. These sins are expressed in words and looks which show that God's kingdom has not yet fully come and render us liable to his judgment.

Having identified the problem, Jesus provides two disciplines to root out these vices and cultivate the virtues of discipleship. We are to be active peacemakers and reconcilers (vv. 23–24; see 5:9) and to be ruthless in our quest for righteousness by eradicating all that leads us away from God's best (vv. 29–30; see 5:6, 8).

3 Following Jesus: ethics as discipleship

Mark 8:27–38

The danger with basing Christian ethics on the teachings of the Decalogue (or even the Sermon on the Mount) is that we can detach the way we live, and how we think about the way we live, from the heartbeat of Christianity, the person of Jesus Christ.

The end of today's passage starkly tells us that Christianity is not about following rules or even rooting out sins and cultivating virtues. Christianity is about following Jesus. Therefore, the first thing we need to be clear about is who Jesus is. The question 'Who do people say I am?' (v. 27) would often be answered today with the words, 'A great moral teacher'. Christianity is therefore seen in terms of obeying Jesus' moral teaching. Such obedience is clearly important—the two houses at the end of the Sermon on the Mount (Matthew 7:24–27) remind us of that—but Jesus is ultimately interested in our personal response about his identity. '"But what about you?" he asked. "Who do you say I am?"' (v. 29a).

Peter's response, however, shows that even simply getting this answer correct is not enough. He had correctly discerned that Jesus was the Messiah, the anointed king of Israel (v. 29b), but he thought he knew what that entailed—even to the point of rebuking Jesus for speaking of his death (vv. 31, 32). Correctly identifying Jesus doctrinally, but then determining for ourselves the sort of Jesus we are willing to follow (generally creating a Jesus we expect to benefit from following!), is a recurrent temptation.

Jesus' rebuke is stark (v. 33) but his subsequent teaching—notably to the crowds, not just the disciples—is starker still. His life is cruciform, and so must be the lives of his disciples. As Paul would later write to an early Christian community, being in Christ means that our minds are to be the same as the mind of Christ, who emptied himself to death on a cross (Philippians 2:5–11). Self-denial and taking up the cross (a sign in the ancient world that you were headed to death because you had been marked as a non-conformist rebel by the powers that ruled the world) are at the heart of Christian ethics. Discipleship means being willing to lose our life and to be shamed in front of the world because we are not ashamed of following Jesus and his words (vv. 35–38).

4 Loving God and neighbour

Matthew 22:34–40

We have seen that Christian ethics is focused on following the one who fulfilled the law and the prophets (Mark 8:34; Matthew 5:17) in a life of self-denial. But how does that relate to the law and how might self-denial be expressed more positively? In this passage Jesus articulates the 'double-love command' that has been at the heart of Christian ethics for 2000 years.

The question asked of him was not an unusual one. Jewish legal experts such as his interrogator often asked which of the 613 commandments in the Mosaic Law was the greatest. Jesus' answer points back to well-known texts from the Law, but his combination of the two in this way is original. First, in verse 37, he quotes the Shema from Deuteronomy 6:4–5. This is part of the prayer recited daily by Jews, which begins (like the Decalogue) by identifying the God we are called to love with our whole being as the covenant God and 'one Lord'. Second, in verse 39, he quotes from Leviticus 19:18, the commandment to love our neighbours as we love ourselves. Although self-love is not commanded here, it is assumed—a reminder that the self-denial of discipleship is not self-loathing.

Jesus' understanding of what such neighbour-love means in practice is best summed up in the wonderfully practical but personally challenging Golden Rule ('Do to others what you would have them do to you, for this sums up the Law and the Prophets': Matthew 7:12; compare 22:40). It is perhaps best illustrated by the parable of the good Samaritan (Luke 10:25–37), which also challenges the idea that 'neighbour' can be restricted to 'fellow Israelite'.

The final verse (v. 40) makes clear that, for Jesus, these are not just the two greatest commandments but are the key to all the others. Some people, working under the label 'situation ethics', have understood this to mean that Christian decision-making is a case of 'all you need is love'. Most biblical scholars and Christian ethicists do not, however, believe Jesus was being dismissive of the rest of the commandments. Rather, he was giving us the love of God and love of neighbour as the interpretive keys by which we can understand what we read in the Old Testament law and how we might live faithfully today.

5 Living worthy lives

Ephesians 4:1–5, 17–32

As we turn to look at discipleship in Paul's letters and the first Christian communities, the opening verse can easily be passed over. Paul's self-description (v. 1) marks him out as someone who has indeed followed Jesus and taken up his cross. The fact that he is 'a prisoner for the Lord' also gives some shape to the crucial description of the Christian life that follows. Paul is eager that the Christians in Ephesus (the request is to 'you' plural) live a life worthy of the calling they have received—literally, 'the calling with which they have been called'. This shows again that we are to think of Christian ethics in terms of discerning and living out a fitting response to the character and word and work of God. That is a key test of any claim to be practising authentic Christian discipleship.

The characteristics of that way of life are summarised in a range of virtues (v. 2), which are closely tied to the unity of the Church, the community in which we are ethically shaped to be and become the body of Christ on earth.

Paul later describes (vv. 17–19) how this way of life requires a break with the Ephesian Christians' darkened, dissolute and depraved past ways of living and thinking. This distinctive life is founded on their relationship with Christ (vv. 20–21) and the fundamental teaching given to new converts about putting off an old way of life where following one's desires led to corruption (v. 22). The positive alternative is not greater self-effort. It is a willingness to undergo intellectual renewal (v. 23) and a receiving for oneself of God's gift in Christ—'the new self, created to be like God in true righteousness and holiness' (v. 24).

Paul sketches some of the practical outworking of this new identity in relation to areas addressed in other passages we have read, which illustrate the pattern of neighbour-love: truth (v. 25), anger management (vv. 26–27), work (v. 28) and edifying speech (v. 29).

The final verses point to the trinitarian structure of Christian ethics. They provide another motivation for such a way of life—God has marked us as his possession by sealing us with his Holy Spirit, whom we must not grieve (v. 30)—and then paint a final portrait of how we shall live if we treat each other as Christ has treated us (vv. 31–32).

6 How to discern God's will

Romans 12:1–2, 9–21

Paul packs an awful lot into the opening two verses of Romans 12. The opening word, 'Therefore', points us back to what has preceded this chapter. It thus reminds us that Christian ethics is the logical and practical outworking of what we know of God's merciful work of redemption (Romans 1—11), and that ethics is to be shaped by our response of worship (11:33–36).

At the end of verse 2 we are told the goal of Christian ethics: nothing less than testing and approving, or discerning, God's will. The fall was marked by the quest to know good and evil apart from and in violation of God's will (Genesis 3:5, 22). Redemption is marked by corporately (the subjects here are again plural) seeking to know God's will, which he has revealed in the Decalogue, in Christ's teaching and, supremely, in Christ himself.

Paul calls us to undertake three tasks to accomplish this goal. First, echoing Jesus' call to take up our cross and follow him, we are unreservedly to offer our bodies in sacrificial self-offering (v. 1b). Here we see that knowing God's will is not simply an academic exercise. Such knowledge is granted to those whose desire is to know the truth in order to live the truth. Second, echoing the call to be salt and light, we are to resist the pressures of our society through acts of wilful non-conformity. In the words of J.B.

Phillips' translation, 'Don't let the world around you squeeze you into its own mould' (v. 2a). Third, in a reminder that Christian ethics is not simply a matter of willpower or intuition or gut feelings, we are called to experience transformation through intellectual renewal (v. 2b). These are the three keys that Paul provides for us to know God's will. Again, they are all corporate, not focused on the individual. It is through being part of communities committed to these disciplines that we will grow in knowledge and Christ-likeness.

Finally, the pattern of the community life that will then be presented to the wider world, including the Church's enemies, is described in verses 9–21. These verses are packed full with echoes of Jesus' teaching, particularly in the Sermon on the Mount, and are centred on the command to love, which, Paul will later conclude, is 'the fulfilment of the law' (13:10).

Guidelines

These selections have highlighted a number of key themes in Christian ethics and discipleship found in the Old Testament and the teachings of Jesus and Paul.

• How important is it for the Church and for British society today to re-learn and re-apply the moral teaching of the Decalogue, and how can this be done?

• A common theme in these passages has been that how we are to live is a response to who God is and what he has done for us. Write down some of the features of God's character; then praise him for them and pray for yourself and others, that you may be better images of this God.

• 'When Christ calls a man, he bids him come and die' (Dietrich Bonhoeffer). What have you had to die to as part of following Jesus? What might taking up your cross and following Jesus involve in your neighbourhood, church, family or work?

• We often privatise ethics today, seeing it as a personal matter for individuals. These readings have highlighted God's call to his people as a community. How does your local Christian community help you and others to become more faithful disciples? What more can be done?

• 'Whoever, then, thinks that he understands the Holy Scriptures, or any part of them, but puts such an interpretation upon them as does not tend to build up this twofold love of God and our neighbour, does not yet understand them as he ought. If, on the other hand, a man draws a meaning from them that may be used for the building up of love, even though he does not happen upon the precise meaning which the author whom he reads intended to express in that place, his error is not pernicious, and he is wholly clear from the charge of deception' (Augustine). How can Jesus' double-love command help us in understanding the Bible?

Almighty God,
you have taught us through your Son
that love is the fulfilling of the law:
grant that we may love you with our whole heart
and our neighbours as ourselves;
through Jesus Christ our Lord.

Ezra

Jerusalem fell to the Babylonian invaders in 587BC. Many of the inhabitants of Judah were taken into exile—but many from the poorest classes were left behind. For nearly 50 years the exile continued, and the Bible has little to say about the situation in Judah during that time.

The silence is finally broken by the account in Ezra, which, with the subsequent book of Nehemiah, sheds light on events from 538 to 432. Here we glimpse the Jewish people during the first 100 years or so of Persian rule. As a small part of the mighty Persian empire, their country is known simply as the province of Yehud (Judah).

The book of Ezra strikes modern readers as rather untidy. It jumps about over a long historical period from one incident to another. Furthermore, it seems to be made up of very diverse material. The first six chapters contain historical information about the early Persian period (the reigns of Cyrus, Artaxerxes and Darius), supplemented by official documents from the Persian court relating to affairs in the province of Yehud. Whoever composed the book of Ezra was able to get hold of these official documents and incorporate them into the account. There are also stories told about Ezra and by Ezra (chs. 7—10). It has often been supposed that there is a so-called 'Ezra memoir', written by Ezra himself, lying behind these chapters. A liking for genealogical lists is also a marked feature of this book. Their snippets of information provide a glimpse into the day-to-day events of the post-exilic Jewish community.

Despite this apparent hotch-potch of different material, there is a common theme running through this book and the contemporary account of Nehemiah. They aim to demonstrate how the people of God survived in the difficult political circumstances of the Persian empire. The editor of Ezra–Nehemiah is keen to show that the return to Jerusalem, the rebuilding of its temple, the repair of its walls and the institution of the Mosaic Law posed no threat to Persian sovereignty.

Similar stories are told elsewhere in the Bible of Jewish heroes and heroines learning to live peaceably in a foreign court or land, despite the inevitable tensions. They include Joseph in the court of Pharaoh, Daniel among the rulers of Babylon and Queen Esther at the court of Ahasuerus. The Jewish people may have strange customs in the eyes of their masters, but they seek only to be obedient to the commands of God.

For this reason, the most likely setting for the final editing of Ezra (and Nehemiah) is towards the end of the Persian period, some time before the conquest by Alexander in 331. This is roughly the same period as the work of the Chronicler, though whether he was the editor of Ezra–Nehemiah too is much debated.

Quotations are taken from the New Revised Standard Version.

1 An unlikely saviour

Ezra 1

Cyrus, a prince of the Achaemenid family in southern Iran, came to power in his own small province in 556. Within less than 20 years, he united the Medes and Persians, and made conquests in Asia Minor (modern Turkey). Finally, in October 539, he captured the city of Babylon. The author of Ezra sees these dramatic events as the fulfilment of God's promises through the prophets. Jeremiah had twice spoken of a 70-year period of Babylonian subjection and had graphically described the fall of the tyrant city (25:11; 29:10; 51:1–58). Earlier prophets saw God using foreign rulers to achieve his purposes—the Assyrian king to punish the northern kingdom, and Nebuchadnezzar of Babylon as his instrument against Jerusalem. In the same way, Cyrus is now seen as the instrument of salvation.

The king's edict is the first of the official documents quoted in the book of Ezra (vv. 2–4; see also 6:3–5). Some scholars think that the version in this chapter, in Hebrew, was the original spoken announcement made by heralds to the Jewish populace. The chapter 6 equivalent is in Aramaic, and may represent the 'official' written document.

The Persian policy of returning exiled peoples to their homeland made good political sense. It helped to gain the favour of these conquered peoples and would therefore diffuse thoughts of rebellion. Cyrus treated not only the Jews but also other conquered peoples in this way. His policy of toleration stood in contrast, however, to those of the previous Assyrian and

Babylonian powers. Unlike these Mesopotamian kingdoms, or Egypt, the land of slavery, there is little animosity towards the Persians in the Bible. For the author of Ezra, Persian rule is acceptable so long as it does not interfere with the Jews' religious beliefs and practices. The Jews must remain distinct and not intermarry with foreigners, but it is possible for them to live in harmony under a tolerant foreign power.

Verses 1 and 5 speak of God 'stirring up the spirit' of Cyrus and of the people, echoing Isaiah 41:2 and Jeremiah 51:11. It is not clear whether the neighbours who give gifts (vv. 4, 6) are fellow Jews or Gentiles. If the latter, this echoes the theme of the 'spoiling of the Egyptians' found in the Exodus story, where the Egyptians gave gifts to the departing Israelites to speed them on their way (Exodus 12:35–36).

The temple vessels, carefully listed in the inventory, represent an important continuation between Solomon's first temple and the plans for the building of the second temple. Amid so much change, there is continuity as well.

2 Passport control

Ezra 2

In the West today, we live in a very individualistic society. It was not like this in the ancient world: your identity was established by the clan or family, town or village to which you belonged. Therefore, this list was not 'boring' for the author of Ezra–Nehemiah. In fact, he found it so stimulating that he included it twice (see also Nehemiah 7). These people, as much as the temple vessels, represented the precious continuity between past and present, before the exile and after it. God's promises concerning land and descendants still stood: he had not gone back on his word.

The list is divided into clear and distinct sections.

Leaders (v. 2): Nehemiah 7 includes an extra name, Nahamani, that has been lost from here, taking the total to twelve leaders. This is an echo of the twelve tribes who took possession of the land under Joshua's leadership hundreds of years before.

Lay people: This list is divided between family names (vv. 3–20) and place names (vv. 21–35). Most of the numbers identified with the towns and villages of this second part are small, in the lower hundreds or even tens. The total of 3630 for Senaah (v. 35) is exceptionally high. Some think it may refer to some specific group or class of people, rather than a place name.

Priests (vv. 36–39): The four priestly houses number 4279 out of the total of 42,360 returners, so more than ten per cent of those returning were priests, eager to work again at the temple.

Levites, singers, gatekeepers (vv. 40–42): By contrast, the number of Levites is very small, and of singers and gatekeepers not much better. This contrasts with the emphasis on these groups found in the books of Chronicles.

Other temple personnel (vv. 43–58): Some of these are foreign names and many are nicknames—for example, Hasupha (Quick), Lebanah (White) and Hakupha (Stooped). Some, like the Meunim or Nephisim, may originally have been prisoners of war, since they are the names of ethnic groups.

Disputed lines (vv. 59–63): The entry qualifications were quite strict and not every family could prove its origins. For the priestly families, this was a particularly serious matter. If they could not prove their descent from the family of Aaron, then they could not act as priests.

Those who return bring with them gifts for the rebuilding of the temple (vv. 68–69). Since there is no longer a king, the second temple will be much more of a community-funded project than the first temple.

3 Making a start and laying foundations

Ezra 3

One of the first tasks of the returning group (in September 538) was to rebuild the altar (vv. 3–6). We do not know if sacrifices had continued after 587. If so, the returning group would consider them illegitimate, because the old altar had been made unclean. The rebuilding of the altar and re-establishment of regular times for sacrifice forge links in the chain of continuity between the first and second temples. These sacrifices include both the daily offerings and those for the appointed feasts: calendars are an important part of religious identity.

The preparations for the building work (vv. 7–9) present us with a historical problem, however. Were they part of the first attempt, in 537, or of the later successful venture in 520–515? Were the leaders Jeshua and Zerubbabel around in 537, or did they come on the scene later? According to Ezra 5:16, Sheshbazzar laid the foundations, but then the work broke off. Haggai, around 520, speaks bitterly as if the temple is still in ruins and nothing has been done (1:4). Perhaps we should suppose that Sheshbazzar started in 537 but that nothing much came of it. The real work of rebuilding clearly did not take place in the 530s, in Cyrus' reign, but only after 520 in the reign of Darius.

The brief description of the laying of the foundation stone (vv. 10–13) echoes the story of the laying of the foundation of the first temple. This second temple is a new beginning and also a continuation. Much of the first temple was destroyed by fire in 587, but a good deal of the foundations may have remained. Think of how many ancient churches have been built and rebuilt on one site. On one piece of sacred ground, succeeding generations build different expressions of the same basic faith.

The celebratory chorus appears often in the Psalms (see especially Psalm 136). Yet some people weep at what they see. For those who remember 50 years back, the beautiful old building will always be 'the temple'. We find a similar response in Haggai 2:3, and the words of Zechariah 4:10 perhaps hold the clue. For all the brave endeavours, it seems to the old-timers that they live in a 'day of small things' and are not the people that their forebears were. However, such an attitude can become dispiriting to all. Religious communities afflicted by melancholy about 'the good old days' often become exceedingly demoralised, and end up doing nothing. Fortunately in this instance the sound of weeping does not drown the positive sound of rejoicing.

4 Fast forward

Ezra 4:1–23

The group offering assistance to the builders (vv. 1–5) are descendants of the settlers brought in to repopulate the devastated northern kingdom after the destruction of 722. No doubt they married some of the survivors of the northern kingdom and adopted worship of the Lord. However, they would have also continued with religious practices from their pagan background. The group from Babylon are not willing to recognise them for three reasons: they are not true descendants of Abraham, but of mixed race; they have mixed true worship with their own native customs; and they are not part of the true 'remnant'. In the language of Jeremiah 24, they are 'bad figs', while those returning from Babylon are the 'good figs'.

The material in verses 6–23 is chronologically out of place, dealing with events in the reigns of later kings, Xerxes (486–465) and Artaxerxes (464–424). Furthermore, the subject matter is the building of the city wall, not the temple. The author is using a 'fast-forward' technique here. Verses 1–5 tell of the beginnings of opposition to the rebuilding programme, while verses 6–23 continue the theme of plotting and accusation against the community of returned Jews in Jerusalem. The pattern described in summary in verses 4–5 will continue for most of the next century. Thus, although this section disrupts the timeline and is out of sequence, it fits the developing theme of our author.

Three separate examples of diplomatic correspondence sent to the Persian court are mentioned in verses 6–8 but the author chooses to give full details only of the third. The opposition seize upon the building of the city walls as a sign of disloyalty. Both Egypt and Babylon had rebelled against the Persians in the previous 30 years, and the Persian governor Megabyzus led an internal revolt in 458, just the point at which Ezra arrives in Jerusalem.

Perhaps the description that Nehemiah hears in 445 about the destruction of the walls and gates of Jerusalem reflects the events of this turbulent period (Nehemiah 1). The cessation of building in verses 21–22 may indicate that the opponents were successful in preventing progress on the walls in the period 458–445. It is often the case that local issues get sucked into the intrigues of superpower politics. During the Cold War, many parts of Africa, the Middle East and elsewhere were caught up in the rivalries between the USA and USSR. Jerusalem and Judah may only be a small area in a huge empire. Nevertheless, Ezra and Nehemiah are treading in a political minefield, quite apart from the religious dimension to their work.

5 Stop—go

Ezra 4:24 brings us back to the main story in the period around 520BC, the second year of King Darius. It is time to recommence the account of the building of the sanctuary.

In 5:1–5 we are introduced to the prophets Haggai and Zechariah. Darius came to the throne of Persia in 522, but for the first two years his great empire looked shaky. A hint of this may be found in Haggai 2:22–23, which speaks of kingdoms overthrown and civil war. The prophets thought this was an auspicious time to relaunch a temple building project: their words had the desired effect, and work on the long-delayed project restarted.

Even in a time of political confusion, there was no getting away from Persian bureaucracy. The sprawling empire was divided into large territorial units called 'satrapies', and the chief administrator of each was called a 'satrap'. At the time of Haggai and Zechariah, the regions of 'Babylon' and 'Beyond the River' (that is, west of the Euphrates) formed one satrapy. The satrap lived in Babylon and his deputy, Tattenai, was located in Damascus. On his official visit to Jerusalem, Tattenai's enquiries are not particularly hostile but he wants to make sure that the work has proper approval. After all, a temple structure might easily be a fortress in disguise!

Once more (vv. 6–17) we have a copy of an official document from the Persian administration. Where did our author get this information? He seems to have been Jerusalem-based, rather than a resident in Babylon or Persia, so the most likely source of his information is from official archives preserved in Jerusalem itself. His other possible source is the biblical material provided in prophetic books such as those of Haggai and Zechariah.

We learn a little about the actual structure of the second temple from Tattenai's description. In addition to blocks of stone, timber is laid in the walls (v. 8). Archaeology confirms that important structures were often built with several layers of stone followed by a layer of timber, probably as protection against earthquake damage. Tattenai includes in his report the response of the Jews to his initial investigations. Their words show that they have taken to heart the lessons of their history (v. 12). The message is clear—the God of heaven and earth is in control of all history.

The elders' words in verse 16 might suggest that work went on continually from 537 to 520. However, as we have seen, the impression gained from Haggai and Zechariah is that work had come to a standstill and that a fresh start had to be made in 520.

6 The king's edict and a new temple

Ezra 6

The decree of Cyrus cited in verses 3–5 is not a word-for-word copy of 1:2–4. It reads more like an official memo than a public proclamation. Note, for instance, that it specifies the exact dimensions of the building, as well as the construction materials. This might suggest that it was drawn up by the king's civil servants, in consultation with the leaders of the Jewish community.

The implication of Darius' decree is that the money for the repairs should come from the tax revenues of the region 'Beyond the River' (v. 8) rather than as a straightforward grant from the royal treasuries, so it is not quite as generous as it seems. Nevertheless, it is impressive that a pagan should encourage the construction of the house of the Jewish God. The Lord of Hosts will receive sacrifices subsidised by Persian taxes! In return, prayers will be offered for the royal family (v. 10).

The comment in verse 14 is significant. The building is finished by the command of God *and* the decree of the Persian kings. The Lord may be over history but all the human actors must play their part. In Christian theology, the debate about divine grace and human responsibility came to a head in the fifth century. The North African bishop Augustine championed divine initiative, while the British monk Pelagius emphasised human responsibility. In the end, Augustine won the day and Pelagius was seen as a false teacher. Perhaps both had an element of truth, and we need to find a way of expressing both views. This verse in Ezra does just that.

The dedication ceremony (vv. 16–18) is marked by the same joy that attended the end of Solomon's building project—but the number of animals sacrificed is far smaller. Only descendants of the tribes of Judah, Benjamin and Levi had returned. Nevertheless, twelve goats are slaughtered, representing the twelve tribes of Israel. The Judean community in this Persian province sees itself as the successor to 'all Israel'. The first festival to be celebrated is Passover, on 21 April 515. There are deliberate echoes here of two previous Passover celebrations linked to restoration programmes in first temple times (see 2 Chronicles 30 and 35).

The final verse describes Cyrus as 'king of Assyria' rather than Persia. The Persians saw themselves as the inheritors of both the Babylonian and Assyrian empires. Two centuries previously, the Lord had raised up Assyria to be 'the rod of my anger' (Isaiah 10:5). Now the same Lord has stirred up Cyrus to be the vehicle of salvation (Isaiah 45:1). Both exile and restoration are part of the web of history, within the remit of the Lord of heaven and earth.

Guidelines

Consider how the return from exile and the rebuilding of the temple might resonate with the issues we face, nationally and internationally, today.

- Do you think Zerubbabel was right to reject the offer of help from the 'people of the land' in chapter 4? How do individuals or communities decide whether it is right to compromise with other groups or not? When are accommodation and compromise right and a sign of strength and when are they wrong and a sign of weakness?
- Ponder your attitude to Christian groups different from your own. Which groups do you work with ecumenically? Which groups do you have no dealings with? How do you make these decisions?
- Many ancient churches are now 'listed buildings'. Think through the issues of heritage preservation, on the one hand, and the desire of a congregation to change its buildings in order to serve the present age.
- Remember those families who in the present time leave one land in order to make their home in another. Pray for those who have to start rebuilding their homes after natural disasters or after the turmoil of war.

1 Ezra's mission

Ezra 7

We must now leap 57 years, from 515 to 458. We have passed from the reign of Darius, ignored the reign of Xerxes, and arrived in the seventh year of Artaxerxes.

Right at the beginning, Ezra's priestly credentials are established. He is, of course, a descendant of Aaron (v. 5) but he has a very high pedigree indeed, being of the high priestly line, with David's high priest Zadok as an ancestor (v. 2).

One of the major priestly roles was to offer and oversee sacrifice. Priests also had a general responsibility for interpreting the Torah and settling difficult cases. Gradually, as more and more of the Torah was written down, the need for literate 'experts' in interpretation became apparent, and the position of scribe or teacher of the law emerged. Ezra is one of the first people in the Bible described as a 'scribe' (v. 6). So Ezra, as priest and scribe, is both a link with the ancient Israelite past and the first of a new kind of figure in Judaism.

Verses 12–26 provide a last trawl through the Persian royal archives. Many features of this decree are familiar from Persian court correspondence. The title 'king of kings' was particularly favoured by Persian monarchs, presiding over a far greater empire than any Egyptian or Assyrian ruler had known. Not until the coming of Alexander the Great would a bigger empire be established in the ancient Near East. The mention of seven counsellors to the king can also be confirmed from non-biblical sources, such as the Greek historian Herodotus.

Ezra's brief is mostly concerned with overseeing the ritual side of the Law of Moses. The administrators of 'Beyond the River' are to cooperate in implementing the imperial decree (vv. 21–24). Limits are set on the provision, but the assistance to the Jerusalem temple is considerable. In addition, all the temple staff are to be exempt from taxes.

The decree ends (vv. 25–26) with a special note to Ezra. His remit to appoint judges in the whole region 'Beyond the River' does not mean that, for instance, every citizen of Damascus would be subject to the Law, whether Jew or Gentile. Rather, the law code is to apply to Jews in every part of the satrapy, not just Judah. This indicates that Judaism was becoming established as an identifiable religious community with a common core of teaching and practice. The heart of Judaism will be found increasingly in the study of the Law as observed in the synagogues, wherever they are in the world.

For the first time, in verses 27–28, Ezra speaks in the first person in his memoir. Later we will find similar kinds of prayer on the lips of Nehemiah.

2 A list without Levites

Ezra 8:1–20

Included in Ezra's memoir is a list of the families who made the journey with him (vv. 1–14). The group totals about 1500 males—a much smaller group than the 42,000 who made the first return 80 years earlier.

The list is carefully presented. It begins with the names of two priestly families and one family head, Hattush, who is of the line of David. Nothing much is made of his royal blood: by the time Ezra was written, descendants of David no longer aroused any real messianic hope. The grand declaration in the last verse of Haggai, that David's descendant Zerubbabel would be like 'a signet ring' chosen by God, had seemingly come to nothing. Dreams of a speedy restoration of the monarchy had begun to fade. Such dreams would not do Jewish–Persian relations any good. The Jewish people were having to learn to use the Persian system rather than trying to break free from it.

Next come twelve key family groups, each introduced with the name of the ancestor from whom the family takes its name—the same twelve family names as those listed in Ezra 2:3–14. This means that, in 538, family groups in Babylon were divided between those members who went home in the first return and those who stayed behind. Now, in 458, Ezra manages to persuade some of the descendants of those who remained behind to finally take courage and go home. Uprooting yourself to go back to a so-called 'homeland' that you have never seen is a difficult step. Dare one exchange the known for the unknown? No wonder families were divided about what to do.

Among the numbers returning with Ezra are no levitical families at all (v. 15; compare the very small numbers in 2:40). Perhaps one reason for this is that the situation in Jerusalem was not very promising: the book of Malachi (from the period 500–450) depicts a dispirited community that has grown lax in its observance of worship and of the Torah. But Ezra is determined to have a full and proper representation of 'all Israel' in his caravan train, and this means including Levites in his entourage as well as priests and laity. After some delay, two family heads agree, at short notice, to pack up and join themselves and their dependants to the emigrants. Together, the families of Sherebiah and Hashabiah number 38 males. Just as the group that left Mount Sinai was carefully lined up in order by Moses, so Ezra, a second Moses figure, can now arrange his caravan across the desert.

3 Towards the sunset

Ezra 8:21–36

The exact location of the Ahava waterway (v. 15) is unknown. Presumably it was one of the network of canals around the city of Babylon. The delay in finding Levites to accompany them has cost time. They will depart on the twelfth rather than the first day of the month (compare 7:9).

Psalm 137 begins with the famous words, 'By the rivers of Babylon— there we sat down and there we wept when we remembered Zion.' Here we view a group of Jews praying and fasting by the Ahava canal. Fasting was practised with increased regularity after the exile. It could accompany rites of mourning or, as here, it could be undertaken before embarking on a difficult venture. What role do you see for either individual or community fasting today?

Ezra is beginning to realise the potential folly of his boast to the king that they are under the protection of God (v. 22; see Psalm 20:7). Now he has responsibility for gold, silver and other precious commodities, as well as human lives. Nehemiah, on his journey to Jerusalem, was perfectly happy to accept the king's armed escort (Nehemiah 2:9). Who was right, do you think—the idealist Ezra or the realist Nehemiah, the pious scribe or the down-to-earth administrator? Is an act of faith sometimes an act of foolishness?

Verse 24 suggests that Ezra chose twelve Levites to have charge of the precious metals. Now it becomes clear why Ezra was so keen to recruit them. According to Numbers 3 and 4, priests and Levites were responsible for carrying the ark and all its accompanying vessels during the desert wanderings. This is a second journey towards the promised land, modelled on the first. Ezra is keen to stress how scrupulous he was with regard to all the treasures, accounting for every item separately as he hands them over for safe transport.

The group departs on 12 Nisan 458 and heads west (v. 31). After about 100 days (7:8–9), the weary group arrives in Jerusalem having covered eight or nine miles per day. A few days later, a much-relieved Ezra hands over the goods to the temple treasurers, two priests and two Levites. Having four men in charge of the temple banking system seems to have been a feature of this time. Twenty years later, Nehemiah will appoint four new people to these posts (Nehemiah 13:12–13). Once more, Ezra insists that he has acted correctly throughout and fulfilled all his responsibilities. Perhaps the memoirs of Ezra and Nehemiah were originally composed as official reports back to Persia, or even as a defence against accusations of wrongdoing.

4 Marriage matters

Ezra 9

The last two chapters of Ezra make uncomfortable reading for those who live in relatively liberal Western societies. There are two opposite and extreme ways of reading texts like this. The first is to accept uncritically our own culture. If we do that, we will sit in judgment on these texts and reject them outright, closing our eyes to what they might have to say to us. The second is to accept uncritically the texts themselves and seek to apply them to our society. If we do that, we let these texts sit in judgment on us and our values. However, to implement such laws in today's 'global village' would be impossible. We close our eyes to what we have learnt more recently if we revert to the attitudes of the fifth century BC.

Perhaps we need to listen to the story itself first, and reserve judgment until later.

One of the issues confronting the Israelites when they first entered the promised land was what to do about the nations who already lived there. The Torah was very strict about 'proper' and 'improper' mixing of all kinds of things. This included seemingly trivial things like not mixing fabrics in a garment, but it also included fundamental things like sexual relations, which go to the heart of both private and community life. Intermarriage with the seven nations occupying the land of Canaan was forbidden (see Deuteronomy 7:1–3).

Ezra has a mandate to enforce the Torah, and seeks to reinterpret the old laws in the post-exilic situation by extending the list of forbidden nations. So he includes groups of foreigners from outside Canaan, such as Ammonites, Moabites and Egyptians (v. 2), which were not named in the old laws.

Ezra's action is swift and very public (vv. 3–15). Like some of the old prophets, he engages in a piece of 'street theatre'. He stages a silent protest in the temple courts until the time of the evening sacrifice at about 3 pm, when he begins his prayer to God. Usually prayers were said standing up (see Luke 18:11–13). It was right to stand straight before God, not to cower before him. However, for his prayer of contrition (vv. 6–15), Ezra kneels in the dust with pleading, outstretched hands to implore God's mercy.

Psychologically the prayer is brilliant. Ezra begins by identifying himself with the sinful people: this is a community sin, not a private matter. Gradually he catalogues the past failings of the people. He quotes from the Law of God and ends with an open question. Will God destroy his people, as he is entitled to do? Or will the remnant survive? The future of the post-exilic community in Judah hangs in the balance.

5 The commission

Ezra 10:1–17

Ezra's public prayer and protest achieve their aim. A sizeable crowd gathers in the temple courtyard, including a large number of women and children. Decisions taken on this day will profoundly affect the family and community life of those present, and future generations.

Support comes from Shecaniah (v. 2), a descendant of the Elam family group. This family had representatives among those who returned in 538, and more have just returned with Ezra (2:7; 8:7), so Shecaniah represents one of the well-established families in Judah. Ezra ended his prayer on a sombre note, but Shecaniah is more positive. He sees hope for forgiveness, and is convinced that the way forward is to act according to the Torah (vv. 3–4).

Unfortunately there are no specific rules about divorcing foreign wives in the Pentateuch. However, Deuteronomy 24:1 speaks of the right of a man to divorce his wife if he finds 'something objectionable' in her. Note that the woman does not have the right to get rid of an objectionable husband! The way forward adopted by the hardliners is to show that foreign wives are 'objectionable' because of their foreign attitudes and beliefs.

Along the sides and back of Solomon's temple stood three-storeyed chambers used for storage and administration (1 Kings 6:5–6). Similar structures were present in the second temple. Ezra spends a night vigil in one of these chambers belonging to a priest, Jehohanan (v. 6). Then everyone in Yehud province is summoned to the temple courts. Since Judah was only about 35 by 25 miles in size, everyone could be expected to attend within three days.

The ninth month (v. 9), Kislev, falls in midwinter. Jerusalem is high in the Judean hills and the weather in December can be quite cold and wet. In view of the complexity of the issue and because of the bad weather, a commission is set up. Sometimes, forming a committee is merely a way of avoiding an issue, but it can also be the only sensible way of tackling a thorny problem.

Four men oppose the majority opinion (v. 15). But what are they opposing? Is it the idea of separations or the plan for the commission? If they oppose the divorce suggestion, they represent the 'lax' party, perhaps having foreign wives themselves. If, however, they are opposing the idea of the commission, they may represent instead the 'rigorous' party that wants a quick decision.

The commissioners take their time (from the end of December 458 until the end of March 457). After all, how many generations do you need to go back to decide whether a person is of 'foreign blood'?

6 Guilty parties

Ezra ends with a list of more than 100 men who were found 'guilty' and sent away their wives and children. This number is actually quite small. Did others refuse to be part of the scheme? What, if any, provision was made for the now homeless women and children? These are legitimate questions, but the Bible simply does not tell us. It is time, then, to return to the question set aside at the beginning of chapter 9. What stance should we take with these painful chapters? Do we say 'yes' to Ezra's policy and affirm scripture, or do we say 'no' and stand against scripture?

If we are to say 'yes', we need to understand Ezra's situation. Today, we are inclined to feel the personal tragedies of Nethanel, Shimei or Elijah and their loving wives and dependent children. However, the issue for Ezra was not the individual happiness of these families but the well-being of the community as a whole. Intermarriage threatened its very existence and its religious basis. Today, Christians who live as small minority groups would understand this well. To marry someone of a different faith community is, in effect, to 'marry out'. The faith is diluted and its distinctiveness lost. If religious structures are to survive intact they may, inevitably, end up hurting individuals. For these reasons we may say 'yes' to Ezra, even if we do not like it.

Exponents of the 'no' position would argue that it is utterly inappropriate to apply Ezra's programme to our situation. That was the error of the old apartheid regime in South Africa. To use the language of 'holy seed' (9:2) today is dangerous and unacceptable.

In the end, Ezra's solution is harsh by the standards of our time—and, indeed, by those of the New Testament. In 1 Corinthians 7, when Paul is asked to advise a Christian married to a non-Christian, he advocates staying together to try to win the partner for Christ. Similarly, Jesus opposes divorce on any grounds (Mark 10:9).

We may conclude that Ezra's solution was right for his own day but wrong for ours. 'Mixed marriages' are an increasing feature of today's mobile society. There are also particular issues in interfaith marriages, where one partner is Christian and the other is Jewish, Muslim, Hindu or Sikh, or has no religious faith. How will the children be brought up? What festivals should be observed? The same concerns arise between partners of different Christian traditions, especially Roman Catholic and non-Catholic partners. When such couples are unable to share Communion, some of the pain of Ezra 10 rises to the surface. Individuals still bear the brunt today, just as in 457BC.

Guidelines

Again, how do the issues raised by the book of Ezra relate to our own time?

- Ezra was both a priestly figure and an interpreter of tradition. Pray for those who offer a sacramental ministry, and those who offer a ministry of preaching and teaching. Consider the place of Bible study in your own devotional life. Why is it important to you?
- Pray for third- and fourth-generation immigrants who feel the ties between the 'old country' and their new homeland slipping away. Remember those who choose to return to the land of their birth for their retirement—only to find that things have changed.
- In your decision-making, are you inclined to act more like Ezra (the idealist) or Nehemiah (the realist)? In what ways is this preference a strength or a weakness?
- Try to get into the mind of Ezra in order to appreciate what was the real problem of the mixed marriages. Reflect on how hard it can be to see things from the perspective of a different culture, time and place. Pray for those who belong to 'mixed marriages' of culture or religion and for their children.

FURTHER READING

For a fuller version of this study, refer to Michael Tunnicliffe, *Chronicles—Nehemiah* (The People's Bible Commentary), BRF, 1999.

Ephesians 1—3

Ephesians is a fascinating letter. It is encouraging for individuals as well as the Church as a whole. Major themes of the book include the unity of the Church, made up of Jews and Gentiles, and the richness of the spiritual blessings available in Christ.

However, it is striking that no specific problem or purpose for the writing of the epistle is mentioned by the author. Paul does not name or greet any individuals, and it appears that the apostle and the majority of his readers had merely heard about one another (see 1:15; 3:1–3). Moreover, in the address line of the letter (1:1), 'in Ephesus' is missing in most of the early manuscripts. All of this has led many to conclude that 'Ephesians' was a circular letter. Indeed, it is likely that the letter was designed for the churches all over the Roman province of Asia, specifically those along the road that Tychicus (see 6:21) would have taken from Ephesus to Colossae, including Hierapolis and Laodicea.

The letter is less specific than Colossians, with which Ephesians shares about a third of its wording. Nonetheless, through the method of 'mirror reading' it is possible to gather what the occasion of Ephesians may have been. The fact that a certain topic surfaces particularly often, like that of unity, may suggest that this was an issue among the addressees. In the case of Ephesians, it is indeed quite likely that the church held factions of Jewish and Gentile believers. Paul emphasises in his letter that Christ's death has rendered this division null and void and has made possible a reconciled and united community held together by Christ, which as a whole enjoys the privileges previously confined to Israel. The unity and the blessings that belong to the Church are stressed so intensely in Ephesians that we have to acknowledge that Ephesians is, in this regard, a development from the so-called 'undisputed Pauline epistles'. However, this need not mean that the letter cannot have been written by Paul (as many modern authors think). It is equally possible that the letter was written by the mature Paul with the help of a disciple. Be that as it may, it is clear that the author of the letter wants the epistle to be read as part of the Pauline tradition, and that is what we will do in the notes that follow.

Unless otherwise stated, quotations are taken from the New Revised Standard Version of the Bible.

1 You are holy

Ephesians 1:1–14

Paul addresses the recipients of the letter to the Ephesians as 'saints' (meaning 'holy ones'). It is noteworthy that Paul uses this description in nearly all of his epistles, which suggests that this form of address is not merely a piece of rhetoric: the truth contained in it was significant to the apostle. However, the introductory section of Ephesians, in which Paul sets out the main themes of the letter, suggests that he has much to say to the particular recipients of *this* epistle about who and what we are in Christ.

In verse 4 Paul specifies that God 'chose us in Christ… to be holy and blameless before him in love'. It is a common mistake to hear these words mainly as an appeal to Christians to live holy lives. While this incentive may be implied in Paul's lines, the main focus of the section is on God and all the things that he has achieved for us. Accordingly, the designation 'in love' is not merely an add-on, indicating that we should be not only holy and blameless but also loving. Rather, in agreement with the rest of the section, and in particular with 3:14–21, Paul is conveying the idea that God's love is the source of our holy life. Only as we experience love are we able to live according to our new status as 'holy' people. We experience this love in the realm of our new relationship to God as adopted children (v. 5) and in our communion with 'the Beloved' (that is, Christ: v. 6).

This love is poured into our hearts by the Holy Spirit, according to Romans 5:5. In this section of Ephesians, however, Paul says that we are 'sealed' by the Holy Spirit (v. 13). This is a different metaphor, indicating that this Spirit of love is the mark of Christians, which shows to others as well as to themselves that they are free and will be free (they have 'redemption', vv. 7, 14). All of this is part of God's larger plan for everyone and everything—namely, to live in close relationship with him. Paul expresses this 'mystery of God's will' as the gathering up in Christ 'to unite all things in him, things in heaven and things on earth' (vv. 9–10, RSV). We will see what this implies as we proceed throughout the letter.

Is your view of our 'spiritual blessings' (v. 3) big enough?

2 Know the power

The phrase 'For this reason' looks back to 1:14, and through it to the whole of what has gone before. Paul gives thanks for the readers of Roman Asia because God has brought them to participate in salvation. He briefly gives thanks, too, for what he has heard of their faith and love, indicating that he sees these qualities as fruits of God's grace. The fact that he knows about them only by word of mouth shows that Paul was not personally acquainted with his readers. While this appears to be of no concern for the apostle, he is clearly concerned for the Ephesians to get to know God more profoundly. The Spirit of God, who in Judaism was often called 'Spirit of wisdom and revelation' (v. 17), is to grant them a deeper perception and knowledge of God (as he is revealed in Christ). On the human side, this means that the 'eyes of the heart' are enlightened (v. 18)—a powerful metaphor for a holistic, existential encounter with the divine.

The result of this intimate knowledge of God is hope—because they have come to see the power of God (vv. 18–19). Power is the main aspect of God's character that Paul draws out in these and the following verses. The Ephesian readers, coming from a background of strong magical belief, might have found the power of Diana more imposing and fearsome than that of God. (Ephesian Diana was regarded as queen over both the heavenly powers and the gods of the underworld.) This could have eroded their confidence in God and undermined their determination to fight in the spiritual conflict in which they were engaged.

Paul knew that the spectacular scale of God's power in his people will be fully disclosed only at the end of this creation, for at the moment our spiritual blessings are 'in the heavenly places' (v. 3). The same is said about the location of Christ's reign over every other power (v. 20). God's kingdom, which is fully realised in heaven, is still in the process of 'coming' on earth. Nonetheless, God's power is 'immeasurably great' for us (v. 19), and it has manifested itself most prominently in the resurrection and enthronement of Jesus Christ (v. 20).

Mighty and loving God, I place my fears at your feet. Will you, by the power of your Holy Spirit, grant me to know you deeper and deeper. Amen.

3 Who dunnit?

Ephesians 2:1–10

In this passage Paul describes a change of allegiance. All of us were, at one point, committed to powers other than God. Here, these powers are specified as 'the flesh' (v. 3) and Satan. The latter is described as 'the prince of the power of the air' (v. 2, RSV), in contrast to God, who is the king of the entire cosmos. 'Air' denoted the lower heavens, closest to the earth, and was often thought to be the abode of the evil spiritual beings.

This state of being committed to Satan and the flesh is characterised as being 'dead in your trespasses and sins' (v. 1, NIV). The fact that 'sin' is thus defined as 'wrong allegiance' prevents us from comprehending it in exclusively moral terms. God is not a perfectionist who is concerned only with people living up to his standards 100 per cent of the time—and in that sense not 'missing the mark'. Rather, as we can see from what follows, God is concerned that we should be in a relationship with him, because of the great love with which he loves us (v. 4).

In the 'then–now' contrast between old and new allegiances, the new relationship is described as one of freedom from the old allegiance. God has saved us. Moreover, he has even raised us with Christ and seated us with him 'in the heavenly places' (v. 6). This location is mentioned here for the third time since the beginning of the letter. Once again, it describes a reality that is already 'real' in the world where God's kingdom is fully realised. (However, on earth this truth is 'proleptic': the complete fulfilment is yet to come.) We do not find such language regarding the believers' resurrection in the epistles commonly accepted as being from Paul. However, it is likely that Paul's emphasis here is due to the prevalence of fear in the face of pagan powers. This is why Paul states ever so clearly that the life in allegiance to these powers belongs to the past.

Not all of us have such a clear 'then–now' contrast in our lives (for example, because we did not become Christian in a mission situation but were raised in a Christian home). However, the way in which Paul ascribes the new life to God is highly relevant for all of us: it is God who is at work in us, 'both to will and to work for his good pleasure' (Philippians 2:13).

What does it mean for our everyday life that God 'prepared' good works for us 'to be our way of life' (v. 10)?

4 The end of hostility

Ephesians 2:11–22

The focus on relationships continues, but now the perspective is widened so that not only 'vertical' but also 'horizontal' relationships are in view. Paul first sheds light on the vertical, the relationship to Christ. Those who did not belong to the people of Israel (that is, the Gentiles) were not as close to God as were the Jews. By employing the spatial metaphor of being far away or nearby, Paul draws on Isaiah 57:19 in order to indicate that the two groups had different degrees of closeness in their relationship to God. However, this difference is now a matter of the past. The peace worked by Christ means that the Gentiles, too, have been moved into a close relationship with God.

However, we should beware of spiritualising this peace, for it has an immediate effect on the nations' relationships with each other. In very drastic language Paul declares that human hostility has been put to death (through Christ's death). A new humanity has come about (v. 15), an Israel that no longer defines itself by separation from other nations but is redefined to embrace all who believe in (Israel's) God through Christ (see Romans 2:28–29; 4:11–12). The law had been like a dividing wall, for particularly the purity and food rules reinforced the separation of Jews and Gentiles (see Acts 10; Galatians 2:11–16). This wall of separation, which had kept the Gentiles away from the household of God as well as from God himself, is viewed here as having had a similar function to the physical barrier that marked off the 'court of the Gentiles' from the 'court of Israel' in the Jerusalem temple. However, this is now done away with (v. 15). Israel and the Gentiles together are now 'God's household' and form a new building (that is, a new temple) on the foundation of Christ (who is the 'cornerstone', Isaiah 28:16). The Church, made up of Jews and Gentiles, is God's new dwelling place (v. 22; compare 1 Corinthians 3:11, 16–18).

Does the reconciliation described here have any relevance for your relationships to people with whom you feel uneasy or unreconciled?

5 Demonstrating unity

Ephesians 3:1–13

Paul refers his readers back to his past, to the moment when he became a Christian. For him, this experience was identical with his call to a new ministry—namely, that of an apostle to the Gentiles. Paul was so moved by what was revealed to him on the road to Damascus (Acts 26:12–18; Galatians 1:11–16) that he started to move in new directions. Paul describes this experience as 'the mystery [that] was made known to me by revelation' (v. 3). 'Mystery' is a term that echoes the language and perspective of Jewish apocalypses (Daniel 2:18–19, 27–30). Typically it concerns God's purposes, which have been firm from the beginning (v. 11) but have been hidden through the generations (vv. 5, 9; Romans 16:25; Colossians 1:26), only to be revealed now at the appointed time, at the climax of the ages (see 1 Corinthians 10:11; Galatians 4:4).

What is the content of the mystery revealed to Paul? The new insight that was disclosed to Paul was the fact that, right from the beginning, God had intended to give the Gentiles a share in the same inheritance, the same body and the same purpose as Israel—'in Christ Jesus' and 'through the gospel' (v. 6). Paul was destined to spread this amazing news. He had devoted his life to bringing the Gentiles this gospel, and thought it worth any risk to foster their unity with the Jewish church. For this reason his imprisonment is for the 'glory' of the churches to whom he is writing (v. 13). However, it is these churches who are the fulcrum point of the revelation, because it is through them that the wisdom of God in its rich variety might be made known to every authority that exists (v. 10).

The key characteristic of Paul's gospel is that God's grace is for all equally and without reference to national, racial or social identity (see Galatians 2:5–16; 3:28). There is a deep challenge here for our Protestant churches today, who so easily split over issues of 'the truth', often without realising that in doing so we are compromising the central truth of the gospel of reconciliation and restoration of unity in Christ.

Do you think that this message of cosmic reconciliation also has a bearing on how people groups other than Jews and Gentiles should deal with one another, even in politics?

6 Being rooted and grounded in love

This is one of the most wonderful prayers in the Bible. It can inspire us in our own prayers for ourselves and others. Paul addresses his prayer (which continues the prayer from 1:16–19) to the Father. In the ancient Mediterranean world, 'father' referred to a position characterised both by power and by intimacy. The fact that Paul specifies that 'every family in heaven and on earth takes its name' from the Father (v. 15) shows the supremacy of this position. In Hebrew tradition, for God to give creatures their names is not merely to provide them with a label but to determine what they are. The fact that God created human beings in plural (man and woman, Genesis 1:27) shows that God himself is relational. What is more, the human family structure is not projected on to God (in the sense of an 'anthropomorphism', as we see in Greek mythology), but God is the originator of fatherhood. He is the 'primeval' father.

The key characteristic of God the Father in our text is that he strengthens the members of the Ephesian churches according to the riches of his glory. How? It is done through the Spirit (v. 16). How does the Spirit empower the believers Paul is praying for? It is through love. The theme of love appears twice in this passage: being rooted and grounded in love (v. 17) and knowing the love of Christ (v. 19). The second occurrence clearly has 'divine' love in mind, whereas the first instance could also be understood as human love. Even then, however, the notion of divine love should not be ruled out, particularly as it is the basis of human love. In any case, the Spirit achieves the strengthening through the relational work of bringing love home to the believers (who experience it in community: 'with all the saints', v. 18). By means of the revelation and knowledge of the love of Christ, the Ephesians are rooted and grounded in love. This knowing of the love of Christ is no 'head knowledge' but an existential, transforming encounter of love, because it 'surpasses knowledge' (v. 19).

Which aspects of this rich prayer could be of particular inspiration for your own prayer life?

Guidelines

We have now read half of Ephesians (and will continue the letter in the next issue of *Guidelines*). It has been a very rich and a very condensed three chapters. In it Paul has unfolded his grand vision that in Christ all things will be united, things in heaven and things on earth (1:10). Key to this cosmic unity is the breakdown of all barriers and the experience of love.

In the case of our relationship to God, we have been united with God through Christ. This is true even for Gentiles, who lacked a family relationship with God (2:19). Now everybody has full access to the love of God. Also, with regard to human relationships, the dividing lines have been erased by the blood of Christ. Together with all other saints, the recipients of Paul's epistle are now in a position to experience God's love together (3:18).

The experience of divine and human love is the basis of human existence. It is also the basis of being transformed and empowered to live in accordance with God's good intentions for our lives together. It is hence important to search for those spaces and places in life where we can meditate on this grand vision and feel and experience the uniting love of God and of our fellow 'members of the household of God'.

While this divine love is always there for us (although it may not always be experientially tangible), the reality of human relationships in this world and also in our churches is often very different. The grand vision of all of us being united by the love of God seems to be totally unrealistic in the face of all the factions in the church and all the hurts that people receive in the context of Christian ministry.

Was Paul a dreamer? Yes, at least on one level—for Paul did not let go of his grand vision, which was already a reality 'in the heavenly places'. However, Paul was also a realist who knew about the challenges of living together. For this reason, the second part of Ephesians is mainly dedicated to ethics. Divine love is never silent in the face of hurtful attitudes or suppressive structures. As we look at the ethical guidance in the remainder of Ephesians, let us not forget that it is only as we are grounded in and empowered by God's love that we are enabled to live this way.

FURTHER READING

J.D.G. Dunn, 'Ephesians', in J. Barton and J. Muddiman (eds.), *The Oxford Bible Commentary*, OUP, 2001, pp. 1165–79.

Andrew T. Lincoln, *Ephesians* (WBC 42), Word, 1990.

I. Howard Marshall, 'Mutual love and submission in marriage', in R.W. Pierce, R.M. Groothuis and G.D. Fee (eds.), *Discovering Biblical Equality: Complementarity without Hierarchy*, IVP, 2005, pp. 186–204.

Max Turner, 'Ephesians', in D.A. Carson, R.T. France, J.A. Motyer and G.J. Wenham (eds.), *New Bible Commentary: 21st Century Edition*, IVP, 1994, pp. 1222–44.

The BRF

Magazine

Richard Fisher writes...

I wonder what comes to mind when you think of Christian spirituality. Do you consider yourself to be on a spiritual journey? Is spirituality something that you associate with monks, nuns or saints rather than with yourself, or with places like a retreat house or monastery rather than where you live? I suspect that many of us wish we had a closer relationship with God, a better prayer life. We look at others and think, 'They seem to be so much better at this than I am.'

'Resourcing your spiritual journey' is what BRF's ministry is all about. We're passionate about making a deeper Christian spirituality more accessible for all of us. While some are called to the monastery or convent, we're all on a spiritual journey of our own, a journey that can lead us onwards towards God and deeper into a relationship with him.

Real spirituality finds God in the mundane and in all circumstances. Brother Lawrence discovered this as he peeled potatoes in the monastery kitchen; Jackie Pullinger discovered it among the drug addicts in Hong Kong. Recently my home group was talking about our experiences of prayer. One person needed silence to pray effectively; another said that they just fell asleep if they were sitting down in silence—they found they prayed best when they were out walking, doing something active. We're all different: one size doesn't fit everyone, and doesn't have to!

What can BRF offer to resource your spiritual journey? Our annual programme of Quiet Days offers a chance to step aside from the busyness of life and catch your breath. The *Quiet Spaces* journal provides articles, reflections and prayers, exploring a different theme each issue; and we continually add to our range of prayer and spirituality books. One to look out for this year is *The Circle of Love*, an accessible guide to one of the best-known and loved icons: Rublev's icon of the Trinity. *The Circle of Love*'s author, Ann Persson, a BRF trustees who regularly leads Quiet Days, writes about the book in this issue of *The BRF Magazine*.

Our prayer is that whoever you are, whatever your circumstances, Christian spirituality isn't something that you just recognise and admire in others, but an everyday experience of your own.

Richard Fisher, Chief Executive

The Circle of Love

Ann Persson

A few years ago I had an eye operation, after which I was required to lie face downwards for a fortnight. Instead of looking at the floor, which was very boring, I chose to have a print of Andrei Rublev's icon of the Trinity placed below me—so for two weeks the icon was my constant companion.

The Circle of Love
Praying with Rublev's icon of the Trinity
Ann Persson

I found myself drawn in to the serenity and harmony of the three seated figures all blessing the cup of sacrifice on the table before them. The longer I gazed, the more engaged I became with the Father, the Son and the Holy Spirit and all that they represent. A potentially difficult experience had presented me with an unexpected gift.

A few months later I was asked to lead a four-day retreat for the Associates of St Mary's Convent, Wantage, and I used the icon as my theme, giving the retreat the title 'The Circle of Love'. Then I was asked to lead a Quiet Day and again I used the icon as my focus. Attending the Quiet Day was John Laister, husband of Karen, General Manager of BRF. He returned home to his wife with the suggestion that the material could be put into book form—and that is how the book came to be written.

> *… the serenity and harmony of the three seated figures…*

It has given me a wonderful opportunity to find out more about iconography, of which I was quite ignorant—its history and the techniques of painting (purists would call it 'writing') icons. It has led to an exciting journey of discovery, central to which was a visit to Russia in the winter cold of January 2009. I went with a friend who is an icon painter, not only to see the icon that hangs in the Tretyakov Gallery in Moscow but also to visit the spectacularly beautiful monastery for which it was commissioned in 1425. This led me to delve into the remarkable life story of the hermit monk, St Sergius of Radonezh, around whom the monastery was founded and who is now the patron saint of Russia.

Rublev's icon is based on the story of the hospitality of Abraham as recorded in Genesis 18. In the story Abraham welcomes three travellers and has a meal prepared for them. However, halfway through the narrative, the visitors become as one and are called 'the Lord'. Iconographers were only allowed to depict Christ, the Son of God who became man. They were prohibited from depicting the Father and the Spirit, so they seized on this story as a symbol of the Trinity and of the hospitality that is not only Abraham's but is also at the heart of the Trinity.

The central part of the book is taken up with a long, slow look at the icon, which is rich in meaning. Icons are not intended to be objects of worship but, rather, aids to worshipping God. They are called 'windows on to the divine'. So it is not surprising that my journey took me into a further exploration of the doctrine of the Trinity, a concept that I, in company with many others, have never found easy to grasp. I was recently introduced to the theory of 'perichoresis' and this has helped me in my understanding. For more about it, read the book! There is a chapter on the invitation to us to become active participants in the life and love of God the Father, God the Son and God the Holy Spirit.

> ... a long, slow look at the icon

I am neither a scholar nor a theologian but I could describe myself as an enthusiast. I am delighted to have the privilege of serving as a member of the BRF council, as I am excited by the initiatives that the organisation is taking to resource the spiritual journeys of all age groups. I enjoy leading Quiet Days for BRF, as it gives me the opportunity to combine my love of God's word with my love of nature. In the pressured days in which we live, it is good to take breaks and give ourselves 'time out with God'. I find that I gain fresh insights and a larger perspective on my life, as well as deepening my relationship with God.

My hope is that the book will serve as a useful resource for anyone who might want to spend some quiet time and would appreciate a theme to work with. At the end of each chapter I have written suggestions for reflection.

It has been a huge privilege to write this book and I am grateful to BRF for commissioning it and to Andrei Rublev for his magnificent icon, but above all to the Trinity who invite me into the circle of love.

To order a copy of this book, please turn to the order form on page 159.

Becoming a more confident Christian

Foundations21
THE NEW WAY TO DO DISCIPLESHIP

Gilly Beardmore

Having used *Foundations21* for over three years, it's wonderful to look back and acknowledge its impact on my life. When I began to use the material, I was able to explore and investigate a lifelong faith in a new, refreshing and invigorating way, which now involves me in a closer relationship with God. This free website has become a routine and flexible tool for discipleship, one that I can rely on to support my Christian journey whenever I need it.

Foundations21 helped me to appreciate the Christian opportunities that God gives us in ordinary daily life. It broke down the temptation to put elements of faith in the separate boxes that are church, prayer, study, work and family. Now, instead, these threads are woven together, revealing God's purpose with a clearer focus. After taking the 'Learning quiz', I was directed to a 'gospel pathway' that best suited my personality and style of learning. I began to travel on a well-signposted journey through the various 'rooms'. Activities encouraged personal reflection; the development of strategies for prayer and Bible study; an acquaintance with key writers, past and present; the investigation and appreciation of diverse forms of worship, spending quality time with God; and an increasing awareness of Christian expression through the ages and into the 21st century.

Instead of being a passive Christian, I gained confidence in expressing faith wherever the need arose and in a variety of ways. I was encouraged, through the contents of the website, to review my Christian life. As a result, faith grew stronger and became a more urgent call on my time. Speed of reaction, materialism, consumerism, image and celebrity, the celebration of the individual at the expense of social justice, and the need to place blame and personal rights before responsibilities—the pressures of today's culture gradually faded in their impact and were replaced with the framework of support that was *Foundations21*. I was gently, patiently and at my own speed invited to examine my relationships with those individuals and groups who were part of my daily life, so that I came to know the blessings of new kinds of fellowship with

Christians and non-Christians whose paths crossed mine. I began to understand more sympathetically the pressures of our culture and how best to express and share the peace that God's love gives us all within it.

Foundations21 also raised an important personal question about the place of humble service. I had to learn to confront humility routinely. I am gradually learning its everyday characteristics through a more patient style of listening prayer—more than I ever did or could before. I now try to listen to God's will and increasingly question my motives before I make choices and decisions. I no longer rely on my own judgment and am more likely to sound out my husband, who is a fellow Christian, and other Christian friends. All these changes have been prompted by *Foundations21*.

I realise that each day invites me to a practical walk with God, which is not always easy and has many unpredictable twists, turns, ups and downs. *Foundations21* is helping me to act in response to opportunities I am given by the Lord. This may involve drafting a list of things to do after listening to the needs of others, or specifically setting aside time to read or pray. I find that I am now more aware of our personal call as stewards of God's creation and, as a result, am trying to improve our household recycling and energy use. Fair trade items appear in our shopping basket more often. I enjoy working in our Neighbourhood Watch alongside other neighbours and local community police support officers.

Foundations21…

is a haven to

return to…

At church, I have been asked to be part of our Children's Church team. Recently, with a 17-year-old, I led a Lent course group and was also involved in another Lent course for children in our town. I have discovered the joy of sharing faith through writing. Before using *Foundations21*, I did not have the confidence to do any of these things and am now more appreciative of the importance of sharing talents and gifts with each other.

Foundations21 has undoubtedly enabled me to be a more confident Christian. It is something I can use very flexibly on a regular basis. It supports me in my attempts to discern God's purposes for my daily life and has enabled me to take part more fully in church, work and family life. It is a haven to return to when I need to say the Jesus Prayer, seek refreshment or simply know his loving presence.

Gilly Beardmore is a devoted user of Foundations21, *BRF's free web-based discipleship resource. To find out more about* Foundations21, *visit:* www.foundations21.org.uk.

Just as at the beginning

Martyn Payne

'Knowledge of the Bible and its stories is declining among people in the UK, according to a survey from St John's College, Durham University. The National Biblical Literacy Survey of people from faith and non-faith backgrounds revealed that as many as 60% could say nothing about the good Samaritan... 62% did not know the parable of the prodigal son... and only 20 interviewees were able to name all the Ten Commandments.' (Source: an internet news report in June 2009)

I wonder what your reaction is to the above paragraph? Incredulity? Sadness? Despair? Of course there are many reasons why this news might not come as a shock. There are large numbers of people in 21st-century Britain who have no contact with church and the Christian faith, so these people will not even be exposed to one or two Bible stories each week in church. There are some religious TV and radio programmes but they are often broadcast at times when few people are watching or listening. Then there are our schools. Contrary to popular Christian belief, Religious Education is still taught in schools, but Christianity is now only one faith among many. Indeed, the new Primary Curriculum guidelines may make it even harder for all but committed church schools to devote much time to exploring more than a few basic Bible stories.

So what is to be done? For the followers of Jesus, despair and resignation are not an option. Rather, this is an opportunity to tell our story with a new freshness—a freshness that might have begun to lose its edge in a more religious climate.

Barnabas Children's Ministry is the face-to-face work of BRF with children in churches and schools. I have been privileged to work with its team of gifted Bible storytellers for over six years now and with thousands of children up and down the country. One phrase from the story of Peter and the household of Cornelius in Acts 10—11 comes to my mind whenever I think back over this work.

When Peter eventually (and rather reluctantly) accepted Cornelius's invitation to preach the good news to a 'pagan' household, he saw the Holy Spirit fall on the Gentiles, just as it had on the first Jewish Christians at Pentecost. It was 'just as at the beginning', as he explains later to the elders back in Jerusalem (Acts 11:15). For us in the *Barnabas* team, telling the timeless stories of the Bible to a new generation of children, it is often 'just as at the beginning'. These are stories that the children have never heard before and our work, dare I say it, has the excitement that those first disciples of Jesus experienced as they set off from Israel to tell the stories of Jesus to the world of the first century AD. 'Just as at the beginning', we see children respond with enthusiasm and wide-eyed wonder as they hear about the people of the Bible who discovered that God made them, God loves them and God has a purpose of love for their lives.

Of course, *Barnabas* Children's Ministry is not alone in this endeavour to bring the Bible to life for the first time for 21st-century children. Like others, though, it has responded to the findings of surveys such as the one quoted at the beginning of this article, not merely as a crisis to bewail but as an opportunity to take.

These are stories that the children have never heard before

Because of your prayers, *Barnabas* Children's Ministry has become very widely known across the UK and is a much-respected part of the home mission work of the church—inspiring, supporting and adding value to the work done by local Christian teachers and children's leaders who share the same missionary zeal. Together we are responding to this opportunity, anxious to make sure that today's children do get to hear about the forgiveness of God as described in the story of the prodigal son, do become aware of the unchanging love of God and his commitment to us expressed in the Ten Commandments, and can respond to the world-changing challenge to love our neighbour with compassion, as expressed in the parable of the good Samaritan.

For more details about our *Barnabas* programmes and how we might work together with your local primary school and church, please get in touch with us by emailing barnabas@brf.org.uk. In this way, we, like the first Christians, can be among those who turn the world (and its surveys!) upside down.

Martyn Payne is a member of the Barnabas *children's ministry team, based in the south-east of England.*

Changes

Jane Butcher

Changes, changes! I imagine that many of us are aware of how things have changed over the years, whether that is in the context of the world, homes, churches or schools. Schools certainly have seen a number of changes, and those who have been teachers for a long time may be able to recall many that they have experienced.

However, one thing that seems to be fairly consistent in our work with Barnabas in Schools is the enthusiasm that children across the country show as they launch into the creative RE Days that we offer. During the course of a day, we often work with children across all of the primary school years from Reception (4 years old) to Year 6 (11 years old). While their responses can vary with their different ages and the location of their school—whether it be urban or rural—there still seems to be great excitement as they explore various themes from a Christian perspective.

Among the themes we offer are 'What's so special about the Bible?', 'Who is my neighbour?', 'Who am I?' and 'Whose world?' Each of the themes gives children a chance to consider the 'bigger picture' but also to explore the part they play in that picture. An important part of the day is allowing children to express their own thoughts, feelings and opinions without being told what to think.

RE Days are led either by a member of the Barnabas team—Martyn, Chris or Jane—or by our expanding team of freelancers. The freelancers are a gifted team of people across many areas of the country who also lead RE Days for us if the location or prior diary commitments mean that a team member is unable to cover them.

Those of us who lead the sessions discover new things alongside the children. It is always an important moment when a child shares something that he or she feels or has discovered, particularly if it arises from their own faith journey. This sharing is not something we expect of a child any more than we would expect it of an adult, but when it happens we feel privileged to be a part of it.

RE Days can be very tiring. They can involve an early morning start to travel to the school, a fairly intense day and often a tiring journey home (for some, contending with the challenges of London city traffic). That said, these times are important in allowing us a chance to share the Christian faith with children and staff, and we gain much, too. These days encourage and motivate us as well as allowing us to keep in touch with the lives of children and what is currently 'in' for them, and to hear about the joys and challenges that they face daily.

The role of RE in the curriculum may change

Another area of work within schools is INSET—a form of training that is offered to head teachers, staff teachers, classroom assistants and school governors. We can offer various training packages, including 'Using drama in RE', 'Storytelling and the Bible', 'Collective worship and reflection', 'Art and spirituality' and 'Using the Bible with children'. We can also lead 'Quiet Spaces', a time of retreat.

INSET sessions enable us to offer school staff some creative ways of delivering RE and assemblies, along with a large number of resources to assist them. We also gain the opportunity to see the world of education from the teachers' perspective and to encourage and support them in their roles, which may at times be the most valuable gift we can offer.

Things may change again quite significantly in the near future. The role of RE in the curriculum may change, which could also mean that we at Barnabas need to adapt our offering to the schools. We would value your prayers as we seek to stay in touch with everything happening in the world of education and to respond accordingly. We would also value your prayers for the days we spend in schools, and particularly for safety as we travel to and from them.

Please do pray for schools—the head teachers, class teachers and other staff who work in the school, whether in a paid or voluntary capacity, and for the pupils themselves. If your local school is close by, maybe you could pray as you walk or drive past. If you live further away, maybe you could set aside some time each week to pray for them.

Schools may be a place of change but they are exciting places where the lives of many children can be shaped and formed for this day and beyond.

Jane Butcher is a member of the Barnabas children's ministry team, based in the Midlands. For information about RE Days and INSET, visit: www.barnabasinschools.org.uk.

Recommended reading

Naomi Starkey

An important part of BRF's prayer and spirituality range are books reflecting the experiences of individual men and women. While books discussing in general terms how to pray or examining different strands of spirituality are helpful, many people find it equally helpful, if not more so, to hear how somebody gained a deeper understanding of God through their personal experiences.

The wilderness is an ancient and enduring symbol of the challenging times through which we may have to pass, just as the people of God did in Bible times. Lynne Chandler's *Embracing a Concrete Desert* shares an unfinished journey through both literal and figurative wilderness places. After moving with her family to Egypt, she spent weary months struggling to adapt to a very different environment. Her book shares her search for a path through struggle and difficulty to acceptance and peace of mind.

Despite the challenges of life in the teeming metropolis of Cairo, Lynne discovers how God can reveal fresh water springs for the soul in the driest of desert places. She realises, too, the importance of choosing to seek wholeness instead of clinging to heartache, and shares what she learns in a series of lyrical reflections and poems. With typical honesty, she writes:

I wish I could say that I have arrived and will never have to stare into the darkness again, but I know that isn't so. I do know, though, that I have to embrace the present moment and celebrate life, whatever that may involve today. My Creator is alive within and throughout this amazing world, and has never failed, through thick and thin, to wrap me in wings of protection and comfort. There are many layers of negativity to be peeled back so that a glimpse of God's image can show through. Just as one layer is lifting, another appears to take its place. That's where grace comes in. In desperate times, God dishes it out lavishly, like my grandma's generous servings of homemade strawberry shortcake.

A different but, at times, equally daunting journey is that of fatherhood. Brad Lincoln, author of *Six Men Encountering God* (BRF, 2008) has now written about what it means to be a dad to his three young children, and how that fits in with his feelings about life, the universe and God. *One Dad Encountering God* does not set out to provide all the answers but aims to get the reader thinking about what really matters.

For example, if we are made in the image of God, our heavenly Father, then presumably there is much we can learn about what it means to be a human father through looking at what God is like. At the same time, reflecting on our relationship with our own children can begin to open our eyes to how God feels about us. As Brad points out, God may have left an important clue about his personality somewhere inside us, as if, in making us, he left his signature. The book is designed so that it can be used as a month's worth of daily reflections for individual readers, but it also includes a section of material for group discussion.

As well as the seasons of life, the seasons of the Church's year, from Advent through Christmas, Easter, Pentecost and on to Advent again, can provide us with a helpful path, leading to personal growth and connection with the rich heritage of Christian history. *Seasons of the Spirit* takes us not only through the four seasons of the year but also through the high days and holy days of the liturgical calendar.

Interweaving poetry and prose, author Teresa Morgan draws on her experiences of ministry and worship in the parish of Littlemore, on the edge of Oxford, to share her sense of how God's love reaches out to transform the world. There are days of encouragement and rejoicing; there are also times when the walk of faith is a weary one. As she writes:

'Watch and pray.' Advent's motto is good for Lent, too. But I am too tired to pray; even the short step into silence seems a marathon. I am tempted to sit down under the chestnut tree and hope that the new life which touches it one sunny morning will quicken me too… We both know and can't know that Easter will come.

In his foreword for *Seasons of the Spirit*, Bishop John Pritchard describes it as 'wise and generous… accessible and full of insight'.

All three of these books offer moving insights into the joys and sorrows of the Christian life as lived by three individuals in very contrasting circumstances. They are books to read thoughtfully and prayerfully, asking God to reveal what we can learn from them to inspire us in our own discipleship pilgrimage.

To order a copy of any of these books, please use the order form on page 159.

An extract from
Working from a Place of Rest

Working from a place of rest

Jesus and the key
to sustaining
ministry

Tony Horsfall

Exhaustion is all too common these days, not least among those involved in some kind of Christian ministry. We can easily forget that there were many times when Jesus himself was willing to rest, to do nothing except wait for the Spirit's prompting, so that he demonstrated the principle of 'working from a place of rest'. Drawing on extensive experience as a mentor, author Tony Horsfall reflects on the story of Jesus and the Samaritan woman to draw out practical guidance for sustainable Christian life and work. In the extract below, you can read the Introduction to the book.

One of the amazing things about the Bible is that you can be reading a familiar passage and suddenly the words seem to leap off the page and hit you between the eyes. All at once the significance of what you are reading bursts unexpectedly into your consciousness, and you become aware that God is speaking to you in a profound way.

It is rather like one of those grand firework displays. There is a bang, a burst of light, and coloured stars begin shooting in all directions. Then another, and another, until the whole sky is lit up. All you can do is stand back and watch in amazement. So it is with these moments of revelation, of spiritual illumination, of knowing something you never knew before. Your eyes are opened to a truth that was previously hidden; that which was obscure becomes plain; and it is not something you are making happen. It is the work of the Holy Spirit, taking the truth of God and making it known to you through the words of scripture. As one truth dawns, another opens up before you in the incredible unfolding process of spiritual awareness.

As one truth dawns, another opens up before you

I enjoyed one such moment some years ago when I was reading

through John chapter 4. I came to the passage in the course of a reading scheme I was following at the time, and I arrived there with little expectation, having read the story of the woman at the well many times before. I was not expecting to receive anything new, merely to be reminded of familiar truths. Then I came to verse 6, and the fireworks began: 'Jacob's well was there, and Jesus, tired as he was from the journey, sat down by the well. It was about the sixth hour.'

In a flash I saw the tremendous significance of these simple words and realised something quite staggering in its implications. *Jesus was doing nothing.* He was having a rest, taking a break, giving himself a breather. Sitting there on the edge of the well, he was pausing and giving himself permission to stop and simply to be.

Then, just as quickly, the thought came to me that *everything that happens in this story happens because Jesus was doing nothing.* The fact that he is resting, taking some time out, is what gives him the opportunity to 'waste' time with the Samaritan woman who comes to the well while he is sitting there. Because of that life-giving conversation, not only is her life changed but the whole Samaritan town experiences revival. None of this is premeditated or planned. It is a purely spontaneous event, dependent on the fact that Jesus is doing nothing.

Christian ministry need not be a matter of striving to make things happen

While I was still trying to get my head around this second insight, a third suddenly arrived. *We can learn to work and minister as Jesus did, from a place of rest.* Christian ministry need not be a matter of striving to make things happen or of straining to achieve our goals through the sweat of our brow. We can learn to work together with God just as Jesus did, for this was no idle moment; rather, it was a moment of communion, of sensing what the Father was doing and of responding accordingly. We can learn to co-labour with God, to collaborate with his Spirit and work in a way that is both efficient and effective. The work is not ours; it is his. If we slow down and take time to listen, he will guide us so that we can share in what he is doing. We can learn to live, to work and to minister to others from a place of resting in God.

I continued to ponder this verse over the next few weeks and months, and to develop my thoughts around the five headings you will find in this book. I have road-tested the material many times in seminars and retreats, and there has always been a good response. People seem to recognise this as something they already knew deep down inside but perhaps did not dare articulate. I continue to read around the subject to gain a broader understanding and I am continually reflecting on my own experience in the light of what I am sharing here, to see if it really does work. I think it does. I offer my thoughts to you with the prayer that they may liberate you into a healthier and more fruitful way of serving God.

The Evangelical Alliance (an umbrella organisation for many churches and organisations in the United Kingdom) met in September 2008 to address what it called a 'crisis in leadership' in the church in Britain. As well as an ageing leadership and a lack of emerging younger leaders, it noted that there is a depletion of leaders, because many drop out through exhaustion and depression.

Listen to what the Spirit may be saying to you deep within

This certainly concurs with my own observations. It is my privilege to work with church leaders, missionaries and key lay people in different parts of the world. 'Exhaustion' is a common word used, and 'tiredness' a number one problem for many. 'Burn-out' is something we are familiar with as a potential threat and, for some, a personal reality. I do not claim to have all the answers and I still struggle myself in some of these areas, but I believe that learning to work and minister in the way that Jesus did must be part of the answer.

So come and sit by the well for a while. Take some time out to reflect on how you are living and working. Watch Jesus and see how he does it. Listen to what the Spirit may be saying to you deep within, at the centre of your being; and maybe, just maybe, God will give you some insights that will change your life and sustain your ministry over the long haul.

Tony Horsfall is a freelance trainer and retreat leader, whose work regularly takes him around the world. He has also written Mentoring for Spiritual Growth *(2008) and* A Fruitful Life *(2006) for BRF. To order a copy of any of these books, please turn to the order form on page 159.*

Tony also leads Quiet Days for BRF. Information about these can be found at www.quietspaces.org.uk.

Guidelines © BRF 2010

The Bible Reading Fellowship
15 The Chambers, Vineyard, Abingdon OX14 3FE
Tel: 01865 319700; Fax: 01865 319701
E-mail: enquiries@brf.org.uk; Website: www.brf.org.uk

ISBN 978 1 84101 554 5

Distributed in Australia by:
Willow Connection, PO Box 288, Brookvale, NSW 2100.
Tel: 02 9948 3957; Fax: 02 9948 8153;
E-mail: info@willowconnection.com.au
Available also from all good Christian bookshops in Australia.
For individual and group subscriptions in Australia:
Mrs Rosemary Morrall, PO Box W35, Wanniassa, ACT 2903.

Distributed in New Zealand by:
Scripture Union Wholesale, PO Box 760, Wellington
Tel: 04 385 0421; Fax: 04 384 3990; E-mail: suwholesale@clear.net.nz

Publications distributed to more than 60 countries

Acknowledgments

Printed in Singapore by Craft Print International Ltd

As a Christian charity, BRF is involved in five distinct yet complementary areas.

- **BRF** (www.brf.org.uk) resources adults for their spiritual journey through Bible reading notes, books, and a programme of quiet days and teaching days. BRF also provides the infrastructure that supports our other four specialist ministries.
- **Foundations21** (www.foundations21.org.uk) provides flexible and innovative ways for individuals and groups to explore their Christian faith and discipleship through a multimedia internet-based resource.
- **Messy Church**, led by Lucy Moore (www.messychurch.org.uk), enables churches all over the UK (and increasingly abroad) to reach children and adults beyond the fringes of the church .
- **Barnabas in Churches** (www.barnabasinchurches.org.uk) helps churches to support, resource and develop their children's ministry with the under-11s more effectively .
- **Barnabas in Schools** (www.barnabasinschools.org.uk) enables primary school children and teachers to explore Christianity creatively and bring the Bible alive within RE and Collective Worship.

At the heart of BRF's ministry is a desire to equip adults and children for Christian living—helping them to read and understand the Bible, to explore prayer and to grow as disciples of Jesus. We need your help to make a real impact on the local church, local schools and the wider community.

- You could support BRF's ministry with a donation or standing order (using the response form overleaf).
- You could consider making a bequest to BRF in your will.
- You could encourage your church to support BRF as part of your church's giving to home mission—perhaps focusing on a specific area of our ministry, or a particular member of our Barnabas team.
- Most important of all, you could support BRF with your prayers.

If you would like to discuss how a specific gift or bequest could be used in the development of our ministry, Chief Executive Richard Fisher would be delighted to talk further with you, either on the telephone or in person. Please let us know if you would like him to contact you.

Whatever you can do or give, we thank you for your support.

BRF MINISTRY APPEAL RESPONSE FORM

Name _____

Address _____

_____ Postcode _____

Telephone _____ Email _____
(tick as appropriate)

Gift Aid Declaration
❑ I am a UK taxpayer. I want BRF to treat as Gift Aid Donations all donations I make from 6 April 2000 until I notify you otherwise.

Signature _____ Date _____

❑ I would like to support BRF's ministry with a regular donation by standing order (please complete the Banker's Order below).

Standing Order – Banker's Order
To the Manager, Name of Bank/Building Society

Address _____

_____ Postcode _____

Sort Code _____ Account Name _____

Account No _____

Please pay Royal Bank of Scotland plc, Drummonds, 49 Charing Cross,
London SW1A 2DX (Sort Code 16-00-38), for the account of BRF A/C No. 00774151

The sum of _____ pounds on ___ / ___ / ___ (insert date your standing order starts)
and thereafter the same amount on the same day of each month until further notice.

Signature _____ Date _____

Single donation
❑ I enclose my cheque/credit card/Switch card details for a donation of
£5 £10 £25 £50 £100 £250 (other) £ _____ to support BRF's ministry

Credit/Switch card no. ☐☐☐☐ ☐☐☐☐ ☐☐☐☐ ☐☐☐☐ ☐☐☐☐

Expires ☐☐☐☐ Security code ☐☐☐ Issue no. (Switch card only) ☐☐☐☐

Signature _____ Date _____
(Where appropriate, on receipt of your donation, we will send you a Gift Aid form)

❑ Please send me information about making a bequest to BRF in my will.

Please detach and send this completed form to: Richard Fisher, BRF,
15 The Chambers, Vineyard, Abingdon OX14 3FE. BRF is a Registered Charity (No.233280)

An updated pack of resources and ideas to help to promote Bible reading in your church is available from BRF. The pack, which will be of use at any time during the year (but especially for Bible Sunday in October), includes sample readings from BRF's Bible reading notes and The People's Bible Commentary, and lots of ideas for promoting Bible reading in your church.

Unless you specify the month in which you would like the pack sent, we will send it immediately on receipt of your order. The pack is free if despatched to a UK address (but if you would like to make a donation towards the cost, we will greatly appreciate it). If you require a pack sent outside the UK, please contact us and we will quote for postage and packing. We welcome your comments about the contents of the pack and your ideas for future ones.

This coupon should be sent to:

BRF
15 The Chambers
Vineyard
Abingdon
OX14 3FE

Name _____

Address _____

_____

_____ Postcode _____

Telephone _____

Email _____

Please send me _____ Bible Reading Resources Pack(s)

Please send the pack now/ in _____ (month).

I enclose a donation for £ _____ towards the cost of the pack.

❏ Please send me a Bible reading resources pack
❏ I would like to take out a subscription myself (complete your name and address details only once)
❏ I would like to give a gift subscription (please complete both name and address sections below)

Your name _____

Your address _____

_____ Postcode _____

Tel _____ Email _____

Gift subscription name _____

Gift subscription address _____

_____ Postcode _____

Gift message (20 words max.) _____

_____

Please send *Guidelines* beginning with the September 2010 / January / May 2011 issue: (delete as applicable)

(please tick box)	UK	SURFACE	AIR MAIL
GUIDELINES	❏ £14.40	❏ £15.90	❏ £19.20
GUIDELINES 3-year sub	❏ £36.00		
GUIDELINES weekly email only	❏ £12.00 (UK and overseas)		
GUIDELINES email + printed	❏ £23.40	❏ £24.90	❏ £28.20

Confirm your email address _____

Please complete the payment details below and send, with appropriate payment, to: **BRF, 15 The Chambers, Vineyard, Abingdon OX14 3FE.**

Total enclosed £ _____ (cheques should be made payable to 'BRF')

Please charge my Visa ❏ Mastercard ❏ Switch card ❏ with £ _____

Card number ☐☐☐☐☐☐☐☐☐☐☐☐☐☐☐☐☐☐☐

Expires ☐☐☐☐ **Security code** ☐☐☐ **Issue no (Switch only)** ☐☐☐☐

Signature (essential if paying by credit/Switch) _____

Please ensure that you complete and send off both sides of this order form.
Please send me the following book(s):

		Quantity	Price	Total
686 3	Embracing a Concrete Desert (L.E. Chandler)	_____	£5.99	_____
710 5	Seasons of the Spirit (T. Morgan)	_____	£5.99	_____
750 1	The Circle of Love (A. Persson)	_____	£5.99	_____
678 8	One Dad Encountering God (B. Lincoln)	_____	£6.99	_____
528 6	Six Men Encountering God (B. Lincoln)	_____	£6.99	_____
544 6	Working from a Place of Rest (T. Horsfall)	_____	£6.99	_____
562 0	Mentoring for Spiritual Growth (T. Horsfall)	_____	£7.99	_____
335 0	A Fruitful Life (T. Horsfall)	_____	£6.99	_____
708 2	The Barnabas Read-Aloud Bible (M. Wang)	_____	£9.99	_____
526 2	The Barnabas Children's Bible (R. Davies)	_____	£12.99	_____
707 5	The Barnabas Classic Children's Bible (R. Davies)	_____	£11.99	_____
530 9	My First Bible (L. Lane)	_____	£6.99	_____
070 0	PBC: Chronicles to Nehemiah (M. Tunnicliffe)	_____	£7.99	_____
151 6	PBC: Isaiah (J. Bailey Wells)	_____	£8.99	_____
082 3	PBC: Romans (J.D.G. Dunn)	_____	£8.99	_____
047 2	PBC: Ephesians to Colossians and Philemon (M. Maxwell)	_____	£7.99	_____

Total cost of books £ _____

Donation £ _____

Postage and packing £ _____

TOTAL £ _____

POSTAGE AND PACKING CHARGES				
order value	UK	Europe	Surface	Air Mail
£7.00 & under	£1.25	£3.00	£3.50	£5.50
£7.01–£30.00	£2.25	£5.50	£6.50	£10.00
Over £30.00	free	prices on request		

For more information about new books and special offers, visit www.brfonline.org.uk.

See over for payment details.

All prices are correct at time of going to press, are subject to the prevailing rate of VAT
and may be subject to change without prior warning.

PAYMENT DETAILS

Please complete the payment details below and send with appropriate payment and completed order form to:

BRF, 15 The Chambers, Vineyard,
Abingdon OX14 3FE

Name _____

Address _____

_____ Postcode _____

Telephone _____

Email _____

Total enclosed £ _____ (cheques should be made payable to 'BRF')

Please charge my Visa ❏ Mastercard ❏ Switch card ❏ with £ _____

Card number: ☐☐☐☐☐☐☐☐☐☐☐☐☐☐☐☐☐☐☐☐☐☐

Expires: ☐☐☐☐ Security code ☐☐☐ Issue no (Switch only): ☐☐☐☐

Signature (essential if paying by credit/Switch) _____

❏ Please do not send me further information about BRF publications.

ALTERNATIVE WAYS TO ORDER

Christian bookshops: All good Christian bookshops stock BRF publications. For your nearest stockist, please contact BRF.

Telephone: The BRF office is open between 09.15 and 17.30.
To place your order, phone 01865 319700; fax 01865 319701.

Web: Visit www.brf.org.uk

GL0210